500 BASKETS

500 BASKETS

A Celebration of the Basketmaker's Art

LARK BOOKS

A Division of
Sterling Publishing Co., Inc.
New York

EDITOR: **Susan Mowery Kieffer**

ART DIRECTORS: **Kristi Pfeffer, Chris Bryant**

DESIGNER: **Jackie Kerr**

COVER DESIGNER: **Barbara Zaretsky**

ASSOCIATE ART DIRECTOR: **Shannon Yokeley**

EDITORIAL ASSISTANCE: **Delores Gosnell, Dawn Dillingham**

ART PRODUCTION ASSISTANT: **Jeff Hamilton**

EDITORIAL INTERNS: **Megan McCarter, Metta Pry, David Squires, Sue Stigleman**

ART INTERN: **Ardyce E. Alspach**

PROOFREADER: **Rebecca Guthrie**

FRONT COVER
Polly Adams Sutton
Onyx, 2004

BACK COVER, UPPER LEFT
Mary Merkel-Hess
Windblown, 2004

BACK COVER, BOTTOM LEFT
June Kerseg-Hinson
Interior Realm II, 2005

BACK COVER, UPPER RIGHT
Dona Look
2004-2, 2004

BACK COVER, BOTTOM RIGHT
Victoria Moran Caluneo
Host, 2002

TITLE PAGE AND SPINE
Billie Ruth Sudduth
Shaker Wall Basket, 2004

CONTENTS PAGE
David Paul Bacharach
Silo, 2003

FRONT FLAP
Gerri Johnson-McMillin
Caribbean, 2004

BACK FLAP
Michael Davis
Textured Vessel, 2004

Library of Congress Cataloging-in-Publication Data

500 baskets : a celebration of the basketmaker's art / edited by Susan Kieffer.— 1st ed.
   p. cm.
 Includes index.
 ISBN 1-57990-731-8 (pbk.)
 1. Basketwork—United States—Catalogs. I. Kieffer, Susan Mowery. II. Title: Five hundred baskets.
NK3649.55.U6A15 2006
746.41'2'0973—dc22
                                         2005024271

10 9 8 7 6 5 4 3 2 1

First Edition

Published by Lark Books, A Division of
Sterling Publishing Co., Inc.
387 Park Avenue South, New York, N.Y. 10016

© 2006 Lark Books

Distributed in Canada by Sterling Publishing,
c/o Canadian Manda Group, 165 Dufferin Street
Toronto, Ontario, Canada M6K 3H6

Distributed in the United Kingdom by GMC Distribution Services,
Castle Place, 166 High Street, Lewes, East Sussex, England BN7 1XU

Distributed in Australia by Capricorn Link (Australia) Pty Ltd.,
P.O. Box 704, Windsor, NSW 2756 Australia

If you have questions or comments about this book, please contact:
Lark Books, 67 Broadway, Asheville, NC 28801• (828) 253-0467

Manufactured in China

ISBN 13: 978-1-57990-731-0
ISBN 10: 1-57990-731-8

For information about custom editions, special sales, premium and corporate purchases, please contact Sterling Special Sales Department at 800-805-5489 or specialsales@sterlingpub.com.

Contents

Ferne Jacobs

Open Heart | 2003

16 X 10 X 10 IN. (40.6 X 25.4 X 25.4 CM)
Waxed-linen thread; coiled

Introduction

Color, form, and texture—especially texture—are what draw me to contemporary baskets. The infinite combinations of materials awaken the senses, please the eye, and challenge the imagination. These are the seductive qualities of contemporary baskets that contribute to their ever-growing allure.

Presented here is an exciting survey of current work exploring those objects defined as a basket by one of three inherent characteristics: basketry technique, traditional basketry materials, or the concept of a basket—as container or vessel. The baskets on the following pages represent at least one of these three aspects of a basket, in addition to being masterfully created and ingeniously conceived. In viewing the submissions, I was continually impressed by the unbound imagination of the artists and their attention to detail.

The term *basket* conjures up images of fiber woven together to form a functional container. Cultures throughout history have created baskets for storing and transporting all manner of items. These vessels ranged in complexity, from basic materials gathered at hand with simple weave patterns, to intricate and delicate artistic expressions, blurring the line between utilitarian and ceremonial. The contemporary basket field today has developed from a merging of two divergent paths—fiber art and traditional basketry. These endeavors have come together to form an eclectic and exciting new art form.

Numerous artists of the mid-20th century turned to non-traditional materials, fiber among them, to create their art. Inspired by the creative freedom of the Abstract Expressionist movement in painting, these artists abandoned preconceived rules in exchange for the emotional impact of the work. It was a natural progression for many fiber artists to move from two-dimensional pieces to three-dimensional objects. Form became a major focus, taking the linear qualities of weaving and enclosing a space. The vessel as a metaphor for containment (even including the human figure) became a canvas for fiber artists.

Flourishing simultaneously with the fiber artists was a new generation of traditional basketmakers. The '60s and '70s were characterized by the desire to return to basics in both lifestyle and art. Artisans were drawn to craft media to replace mass produced items with handmade objects of meaning and individuality. Many followed the lead of Native American and folk craft traditions by using natural materials and established basketry techniques. These two major influences in the field of contemporary basketry have resulted in a widely diverse body of work, spanning the spectrum from vessel to pure sculptural form.

Many artists were important to the growth of contemporary basketry. Each, in his/her own way, influenced the direction of the field; each broke with tradition, pushing the limits of the strictly defined basket and venturing into the art world.

The person most often spoken of as the father of contemporary baskets is Ed Rossbach. By investigating new materials, he broadened the vocabulary of generations of basketmakers. Reflecting the culture of his time, he combined commonplace elements to

Ed Rossbach
Pale Yellow & Rags

13 X 9 X 8³/₄ IN. (33 X 22.9 X 22.2 CM)
Wood, paint, rags
COURTESY OF ARKANSAS ARTS CENTER FOUNDATION COLLECTION
GIFT FROM THE DIANE AND SANDY BESSER COLLECTION, 1997

Lillian Elliott and Pat Hickman
Basket | 1986

23 1/2 X 20 1/2 X 22 IN. (59.7 X 52.1 X 55.9 CM)
Fabricated wood, gut, paint, string

COURTESY OF ARKANSAS ARTS CENTER FOUNDATION COLLECTION
GIFT FROM THE DIANE AND SANDY BESSER COLLECTION, 1992

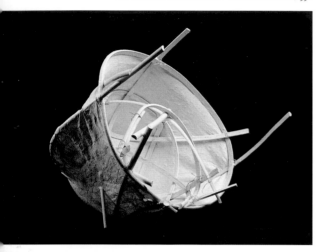

create familiar forms in a very uncommon way. Also stretching the definition of suitable basketry material are Pat Hickman, Katherine Westphal, John Garrett, and Karyl Sisson. Michael Davis draws on his degrees in ceramics and painting and alters the surfaces of his baskets, moving them even further toward canvas.

These artists paved the way for a new generation of basketmakers, many of whose works are seen in this book. Rob Dobson and Aaron Kramer reflect their concerns about our environment by working with recycled materials. Jill Nordfors Clark and Jan Hopkins use the ancient, yet unusual, materials of hog gut and orange peels. Even further from tradition, Lindsay Ketterer Rais incorporates bleached pistachio shells as adornment, and Jenniifer Maestre constructs baskets from colored pencils.

Ferne Jacobs' early coiled and twined vessels inspired others to create basketry; her work has since evolved into pure sculptural form. The work of Lillian Elliott exemplifies the path of a fiber artist who turned to baskets. She believed that basketry allowed her to be more spontaneous and achieve results more quickly than weaving did. Kay Sekimachi, known for her monofilament hangings, paper constructions, vessels of desiccated leaves, and even hornets' nests, still considers herself a fiber artist but has been recognized as a basketmaker for her three-dimensional creations.

Kay Sekimachi
Chawan with Lid & Bowl

5 1/2 X 5 1/2 IN. (14 X 14 CM) DIAMETER
Old Japanese document, ogura lace, India ink

PHOTO BY DAVID PETERS

Dorothy Gill Barnes, Gyöngy Laky, and John McQueen have taken natural material at its literal meaning and brought unfinished branches, twigs, and bark into the lexicon of art.

Jane Sauer shifted from painting to fiber and used pigments on her knotted structures to reflect the mood of the piece. Patti Lechman and Jan Buckman integrate pattern and design onto the surfaces of their twined and knotted vessels. The figurative works of Judy Mulford, Carol Eckert, and Mary Giles, constructed with traditional basketry techniques, express allegorical stories and personal statements about life and our culture.

The baskets depicted in this book vary widely, from artists who have played a major role in the field, influencing many others, to emerging artists whose technical ability and ingenuity have earned them recognition. Some hearken back to original use, while others do not look like the conventional picture of a basket at all, but whether in concept, technique, or form, they make the connection to the long and ever-evolving story of basketmaking.

Jan Peters

Dorothy Gill Barnes
Rally Spruce | 1989

12 X 29^1/2 X 31 IN. (30.5 X 75 X 78.7 CM)
Plaited-spruce bark

COURTESY OF ARKANSAS ARTS CENTER FOUNDATION COLLECTION
GIFT FROM THE DIANE AND SANDY BESSER COLLECTION, 1992

Victoria Moran Caluneo

French Knot Bowl, Timeline Series | 2003

8½ X 6½ INCHES (21.6 X 16.5 CM)

Copper electrical wire; hand-wrapped wire base, coiled, twist-tied construction with knots

PHOTOS © ARTIST

THIS COLOR *combination was my transitional piece when I first became inspired to embellish my baskets all over with curls. It continues to be one of my most popular designs. This work is a signature piece for me. The curl embellishments are a second layer added on top of the weaving below.*

Patti Quinn Hill

Midas Touch | 2005

7 X 9½ INCHES (17.8 X 24.1 CM)

Cotton archival paper, acrylic paint, metallic thread; hand painted, continuous construction, double woven, curl embellishments

PHOTOS © ARTIST

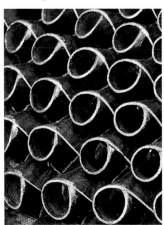

MY CREDIT
*card "beads"
are today's version
of African trade
beads; they are our
form of materialism.*

Barbara Schulman
Artifact of Materialism | 2000

15½ X 17½ X 12½ INCHES (39.4 X 44.5 X 31.8 CM)
Hand-dyed industrial-wool felt, credit card fragments,
linen thread; pieced, shaped, embroidered

PHOTOS © ROBERT WALCH

THIS WAS *the first basket where I applied dapped, copper disks on the surface of a wrapped form. I was looking at acorn caps that had fallen from our oak tree, and I was creating very literal branch baskets in copper wire. This cup form was intriguing, and, as I began to explore ways in which to attach it to the basket, I drew once again upon my interest in fiber arts, and stitched the "buttons" to the surface.*

Victoria Moran Caluneo
Host | 2002

7 X 12 INCHES (17.8 X 30.5 CM)
Copper electrical wire, copper sheet, patina, pigment; hand-wrapped wire base, coiled construction

Victoria Moran Caluneo

Agua | 2004

8 X 7 INCHES (20.3 X 17.8 CM)
Copper wire, sheet metal, patina,
pigment; coiled, stitched
PHOTO © ARTIST

David Paul Bacharach

Tea Bowl XI | 2004

9 X 9 X 9 INCHES (22.9 X 22.9 X 22.9 CM)
Copper sheet; cut, plaited, patinated
PHOTO © NORMAN WATKINS

Sally Shore

Planes and Forest | 2003

4½ X 9 X 9½ INCHES (11.4 X 22.9 X 24.1 CM)

Double-faced satin ribbon;
tri-axial weaving

PHOTOS © ARTIST

Jerry Bleem

Coast: (Rowing to Sexton's Island) | 2002

13¾ X 16¼ X 15¾ INCHES (34.9 X 41.3 X 40 CM)

Found maps and blueprints, acetate, wax, acrylic
medium, epoxy, staples; accretion by stapling

PHOTOS © TOM VAN EYNDE

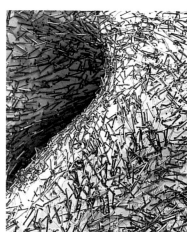

THIS IS *one in a series of pieces made from the scales of an invasive, non-native fish that is changing the eco-system. Though the scales themselves are lovely, they also sig-nal a major change of which most people are unaware.*

Jerry Bleem

Dive | 2002

10¾ X 12 X 8 INCHES
(27.3 X 30.5 X 20.3 CM)
Fish scales, staples;
accretion by stapling
PHOTO © TOM VAN EYNDE

Dennis Nahabetian

Nine-Month Nest | 2003

7½ X 5 X 5 INCHES (19.1 X 12.7 X 12.7 CM)

Copper, bronze, patina with polychrome;
metalsmithing and textile techniques

PHOTO © ARTIST

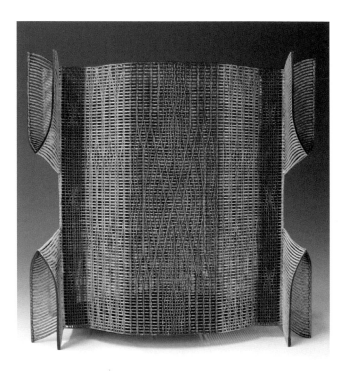

Dennis Nahabetian

Vessel #66 | 2004

7 X 7 X 5 INCHES (17.8 X 17.8 X 12.7 CM)

Copper, bronze, patina with polychrome;
metalsmithing and textile techniques

PHOTO © ARTIST

Helen Shirk

Commemorative Cup V | 2000

21 X 7 X 7 INCHES (53.3 X 17.8 X 17.8 CM)

Copper wire and sheet, colored pencils; soldered, woven, patinated, colored

PHOTOS © ARTIST

Leslee Ann Burtt

Caribou Antler Basket | 2003

30 X 40 X 24 INCHES (76.2 X 101.6 X 61 CM)

Caribou antler, seagrass, reed,
wild-cherry bark; ribbed

PHOTO © BILL BACHHUBER

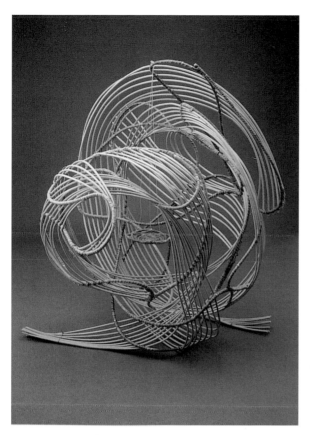

Kinu Watanabe

Swirl | 2004

13 X 9 X 12 INCHES (33 X 22.9 X 30.5 CM)
Reed, raffia, clear wire; hand dyed,
coiled, twined
PHOTO © KATHERYN HARRIS

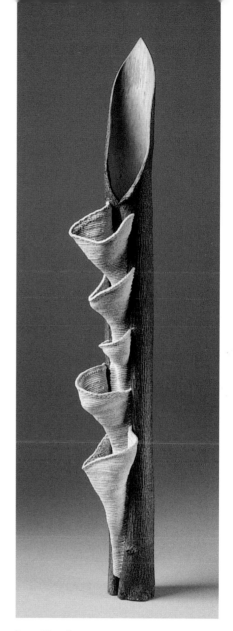

Jan Buckman

Conversion V | 2002

21 X 3 X 3 INCHES (53.3 X 7.6 X 7.6 CM)
Waxed linen, hickory bark; twined
PHOTO © PETER LEE

MY OBSESSIVE *nature draws me to the repetitive looping of knotless netting. I choose to work in wire because of the way that wire holds its shape. I am able to create volume out of very delicate material with relative ease. The stability of the wire also allows every loop and curve of the netting to remain in clear view. One piece informs the next and the cycle repeats.*

Lindsay Ketterer Rais

Neckline Basket | 2004

19 X 18 X 12 INCHES (48.3 X 45.7 X 30.5 CM)

Stainless-steel mesh, pistachio shells, silver and coated-copper wire, aluminum, beads; formed, stitched, knotless-netting embellishment

PHOTOS © D. JAMES DEE

Barbara Shapiro
Not for All the Tea in China | 2003

6½ X 7½ X 7½ INCHES (16.5 X 19.1 X 19.1 CM)
Waxed linen, wire, beads, Chinese antique coins; painted, coiled
PHOTO © SHARON RISEDORPH

Kathey Ervin
Black and Red Button Basket | 2003

10 X 9 X 9 INCHES (25.4 X 22.9 X 22.9 CM)
Western red-cedar bark, Alaskan yellow-cedar bark, antique mother-of-pearl buttons; dyed, continuous twill pattern, woven, twined
PHOTO © ARTIST

Jane Sauer

Endear/Endure | 2001

18 X 10 X 14 INCHES
(45.7 X 25.4 X 35.6 CM)

Waxed-linen thread, pigment

PHOTO © WENDY MCEAHERN
COURTESY DEL MANO GALLERY

I AM *interested in the viewer's interaction with a piece of artwork. The randomly woven vessel can be removed to reveal a reward or surprise for the viewer. I think of this body of work like a new relationship. When you meet someone, you learn a few things about that person, but if you get to know the person better, more is revealed; secrets are told.*

Jo Stealey
Meditation Bowl III | 2004

6 X 9 X 9 INCHES (15.2 X 22.9 X 22.9 CM)
Reed, cast- and pulp-painted handmade
paper, rock, colored pencils; machine
stitched, random weave

PHOTO © PETER ANGER

Edit Meaklim

Segmented Vessel | 2003

12⁹⁄₁₆ X 7¹⁄₁₆ X 5⁷⁄₈ INCHES (32 X 18 X 15 CM)
Polished jute, nylon cord; coiled construction, line stitch

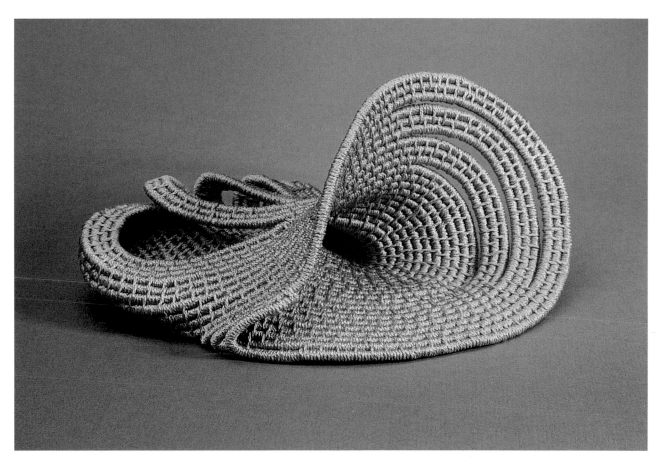

Edit Meaklim

Inside Out | 2003

7⅞ X 5¹⁵⁄₁₆ X 3¹⁵⁄₁₆ INCHES (20 X 15 X 10 CM)

Polished jute, nylon cord; coiled construction, line stitch

PHOTO © GLENN FACEY

THIS SERIES *honors bamboo-basket artists. Inspiration to create, cast, and weave thin splint-like spokes is from a trip to Japan.*

Polly Adams Sutton

Jo | 2005

13¼ X 9 X 26 INCHES (35 X 22.9 X 66 CM)
Cedar bark, ash, wire, cane; woven, twined
PHOTO © BILL WICKETT

Suzye Ogawa

Homage | 2004

½ X 1½ X 1½ FEET (15.2 X 45.7 X 45.7 CM)
Bronze, raffia; lost-wax cast, twined raffia
PHOTO © GEORGE POST

Gayna Uransky

Untitled | 1998

20 X 12 X 9 INCHES (50.8 X 30.5 X 22.9 CM)

Queen palm seed strands, pygmy-date palm
seed strands, driftwood; coiled

PHOTO © GEORGE POST

Risë Andersen

Companions | 2005

14 X 6 X 3 INCHES (35.6 X 15.2 X 7.6 CM)

Rattan, wood; twined using
personal techniques

PHOTOS © LARRY SANDERS

THIS YIN *and yang pairing is the first in a series. The found wood dictated the need for the two halves forming a whole. The weaving became the core—or soul—of the piece.*

Risë Andersen

Pairing | 2004

8 X 5 X 3 INCHES (20.3 X 12.7 X 7.6 CM)

Rattan, wood, dye; personal twining techniques

PHOTO © LARRY SANDERS

Charlotte L. Thorp

Rose Collar | 2004

8 X 9 X 7 INCHES (20.3 X 22.9 X 17.8 CM)

Hand-spun paper spokes, waxed-linen thread, leather cord; twined

PHOTO © D. JAMES DEE

A NON-TRADITIONAL *vessel, exploring bold contrast qualities—tight/loose, smooth/rough, flat/deep, thick/thin. The paper spokes burst from the tightly woven surface with unpredictable and exciting spontaneity.*

Charlotte L. Thorp

Quiet for Now | 2002

5 X 6 X 7 INCHES (12.7 X 15.2 X 17.8 CM)

Hand-spun paper spokes, waxed-linen thread, leather cord; twined

PHOTO © D. JAMES DEE

Doris Messick

Friends | 2003

40 X 12 X 36 INCHES (101.6 X 30.5 X 91.4 CM)
Osier dogwood, copper wire, clay,
paper pulp, glue; twined, coated
PHOTO © ARTIST

Patti Lechman

Sun and Waves | 2005

5½ X 6 X 3 INCHES (14 X 15.2 X 7.6 CM)
Nylon and glass beads; knotted

PHOTOS © ARTIST

I **HAVE** *always loved graphic elements, especially polka dots. I embellished a teapot shape with a playful polka-dotted pattern, bouncing bright colors off each other to create a lively sense of comfort and whimsy—like having a cup of tea with the Mad Hatter.*

Merrill Morrison

A Spot of Tea | 2000

6½ X 6½ INCHES (16.5 X 16.5 CM)
Waxed linen, glass beads; knotted

PHOTO © TRACY TALBERT AND MICHAEL LARSEN

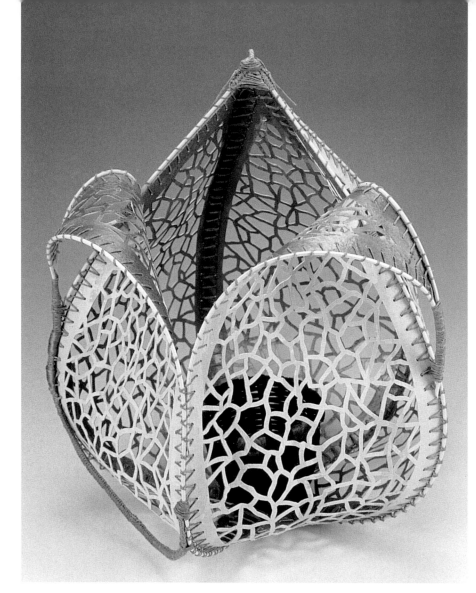

Jennifer Falck Linssen
Open Up | 2005

12 X 10 INCHES (30.5 X 25.4 CM)
Cotton paper, ash, waxed linen, reed, cotton thread,
steel, dye, paint; katazome-style hand-carved paper,
stitched construction, plaited

PHOTOS © AZAD

Dona Look

#2004–5 | 2004

13 X 13¼ X 13¼ INCHES (33 X 35 X 35 CM)
White birch bark, waxed-silk thread;
sewn, partially wrapped

PHOTO © SUSAN EINSTEIN

IN THIS *work I tried to express how something as strong and powerful as the wind can either be destructive or, in this case, press and contort the pine into an object of refined beauty, reflecting both delicacy and strength.*

Jennifer Falck Linssen
Wind in the Pines | 2003

23½ X 15 X 5 INCHES (59.7 X 38.1 X 12.7 CM)
Japanese printmaking papers, reed, waxed linen, wheat starch, coated copper wire; katazome-style hand-carved paper (hikibori), plaited construction, laminated, stitched

PHOTO © AZAD

Barbara Knutson

Ginkgo Leaf Basket | 2004

5 X 9 X 19 INCHES (12.7 X 22.9 X 48.3 CM)

White and brown stoneware, ginkgo leaf cutouts,
extruded coils; fired in gas kiln, cone 10 reduction

PHOTO © RANDY BATISTA

Kay Sekimachi

Leaves | 1998

5 X 7½ INCHES DIAMETER (12.7 X 19.11 CM)

Big-leaf maple

PHOTO © DAVID PETERS
COURTESY DEL MANO GALLERY

Mary Babcock

Untitled | 2004

6 X 5 X 5 INCHES (15.2 X 12.7 X 12.7 CM)

Vellela vellela (by-the-wind sailor jellyfish),
seaweed, microfilament; hand stitched

PHOTO © ARTIST

Saaraliisa Ylitalo

Festered | 1995

14 X 18 X 13 INCHES (35.6 X 45.7 X 33 CM)

Handmade gampi paper, gold leaf, wire; mixed media

PHOTOS © KOICHI NISHIMURA

PLAYFULNESS AND *a sense of liberation*
are elements I try to incorporate in my work.

Stephane Threlkeld

Loop de Loop | 2001

7 1/16 X 5 7/8 X 5 7/8 INCHES (18 X 15 X 15 CM)

Copper wire; rolled flat, straight plaited, patinated

PHOTO © HAP SAKWA

Pamela Morris Thomford

Vacancy: Homage to an Empty Nest | 2004

5 X 6 X 3 INCHES (12.7 X 15.2 X 7.6 CM)

Sterling silver, dyed plastic, feathers, beads; hand
fabricated, riveted

PHOTO © KEITH MEISER

Yohko Kubo

A Form Is Taken (Le Lectier: Silver) | 2003

5⅛ X 3⅛ X 3⅛ INCHES (13 X 8 X 8 CM)

Paper, knitting yarn; coiled

PHOTO © JUNICHI MIURA

Pat Bramhall

Truly Charlotte's | 2002

3½ X 3¼ INCHES (8.9 X 8.3 CM)

Fine and sterling silver; woven, black-ash cannon-points technique

PHOTO © BUTCH BRAMHALL

THESE WORKS *of love, hand woven of sterling silver, were inspired by my respect for wood-splint and sweetgrass baskets of the past.*

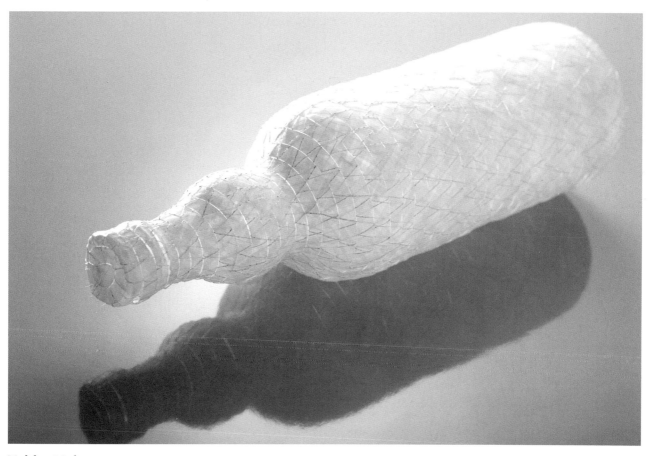

Yohko Kubo

A Form Is Taken (Bottle: White) | 2003

10⁷⁄₁₆ X 3 X 3 INCHES (26.5 X 7.5 X 7.5 CM)

Tracing paper, knitting yarn; coiled

PHOTO © JUNICHI MIURA

VACATIONS WITH *underwater divers are*
the inspiration for my underwater pieces.

JoAnn Baumann

Sea Scape | 1995

5 X 7 X 7 INCHES (12.7 X 17.8 X 17.8 CM)

Seed beads, thread; off-loom bead woven

PHOTOS © ARTIST

Linda Smith

Stream Song | 2003

2½ X 5 X 6 INCHES (6.4 X 12.7 X 15.2 CM)

Glass seed beads, beading thread, shell, abalone, Alaska coral, pearls, lapis, glass lamp-worked bead, fossil coral, turquoise, jasper; freeform bead-weaving techniques, peyote stitch, right-angle weave, netting

PHOTOS © CHRIS AREND

Donna Kaplan

Watching for Whales | 2004

16¼ X 8 X 5½ INCHES (41.3 X 20.3 X 14 CM)

Wire, silk, rayon; loom woven, sculpted, sewn

PHOTOS © MICHELLE BATES

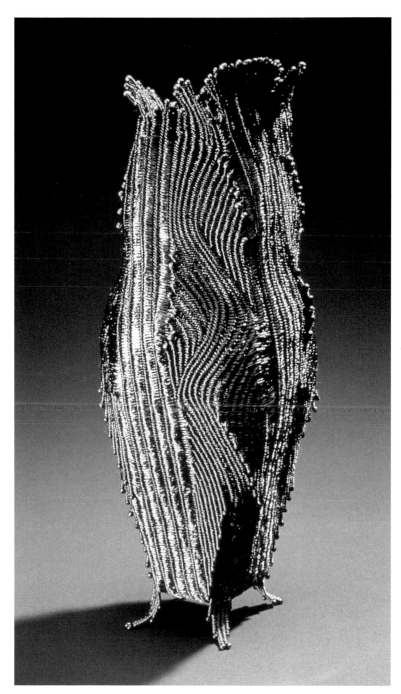

Marilyn Moore

Sapphire | 2005

11 ½ X 5 X 5 INCHES (29.2 X 12.7 X 12.7 CM)

Polynylon-coated copper wire, silver-plated wire over copper wire, copper strips; two-strand twining

PHOTOS © ROBERT VINNEDGE

Cindy Wrobel

Wine Vessel | 2004

8½ X 5½ X 8 INCHES (21.6 X 14 X 20.3 CM)

Beads, wire; strung, wrapped

PHOTOS © JIM SOKOLIK

I **THINK** *of the folded individual units as stitches, and I use these connected stitches as one would use coils in a clay pot. I love that I can control and manipulate the color and shape of my pieces. I also love that I have to surrender to the random designs and limitations of the cardboard.*

Amy Lipshie

Amphora | 2004-2005

27 X 22 X 22 INCHES (68.6 X 55.9 X 55.9 CM)
Cereal boxes, beads, glue, nylon thread, polymer
varnish; cut, folded, chained, glued, sewn

PHOTOS © LINDA JEUB

Carol Eckert

Dual Oracles | 2002

9½ X 13 X 3 INCHES (24.1 X 33 X 7.6 CM)

Cotton over wire; coiled

PHOTO © W. SCOTT MITCHELL

Carol Eckert

Ancient Spirits | 2005

13½ X 1½ X 3½ INCHES (34.3 X 29.2 X 8.9 CM)

Cotton over wire; coiled

PHOTO © W. SCOTT MITCHELL

Rev. Wendy Ellsworth

Tematangi | 2002

4½ X 5 X 4½ INCHES (11.4 X 12.7 X 11.4 CM)

Glass seed beads, wire, thread; off-loom bead weaving, herringbone stitch, gourd stitch

PHOTO © DAVID ELLSWORTH

Brian Jewett

Small Wall Anemone | 2004

12 X 12 X 12 INCHES (30.5 X 30.5 X 30.5 CM)

Plastic tube, cable ties; coiled construction

PHOTO © BRIAN FORREST

Ti de L'Arbre

Royal Blue Granary | 2003

10 X 18 INCHES (25.4 X 45.7 CM)
Wood base, flat oval reed, peacock
feathers; dyed, woven, twined

PHOTO © KENJI

Dorothy McGuinness

Green Tea | 2005

5 X 4 X 5 INCHES (12.7 X 10.2 X 12.7 CM)

Watercolor paper, acrylic paint, waxed linen,
ribbon; broken-square twill start,
diagonal twill, sewn, knotted

PHOTOS © KEN RAVE

Dawn Walden

Turning Point | 2003

20 X 12 X 12 INCHES (50.8 X 30.5 X 30.5 CM)
Black ash, cedar bark and roots
PHOTO © JERRY MCGUIRE

Patti Quinn Hill

Luminosity | 2004

17 X 14 INCHES (43.2 X 35.6 CM)

Cotton archival paper, acrylic paint, maple base, metallic thread; continuous construction, double woven, curl embellishments

PHOTOS © ARTIST

June Kerseg-Hinson

Entropic Plinth II | 2004

18½ X 5 X 5 INCHES (47 X 14 X 14 CM)

Hand-spun kozo paper, copper magnet wire, acrylic paint, pigment, glass beads, steel wire armature; loom-warped knotted netting, interlaced, wrapped, folded

PHOTOS © BILL SMYTHE

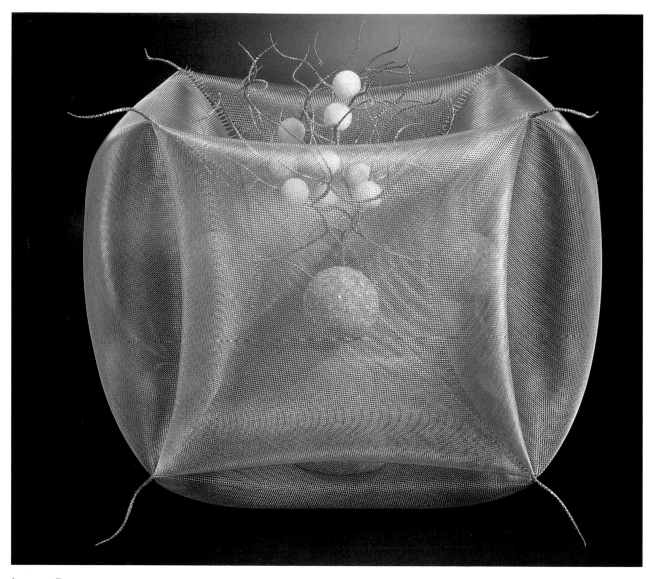

Lanny Bergner

Folding Space: Botanical 2 | 2004

22 X 20 X 20 INCHES (55.9 X 50.8 X 50.8 CM)

Bronze screen, glass frit, wire; connected,
glued, wire wrapped

PHOTO © WILLIAM WICKETT

Debbie Shriver

Lemon Meringue Pie | 2001

3 X 3 X 3 INCHES (7.6 X 7.6 X 7.6 CM)
Raffia, melon seeds; twined
PHOTO © DAVID PETERS

Debbie Shriver

Magneto Electric | 2001

2 X 2 X 2 INCHES (5.1 X 5.1 X 5.1 CM)
Raffia, copper braid, copper; twined
PHOTO © DAVID PETERS

I OPEN and shape the bark fiber to create space for the light to pass through and expose the structure that holds it together. That process involves working with the natural qualities of the bark to transform its appearance and reorder its dimensions. I delight in the paradox that often results—a delicate translucency contrasted with the actual strength and rough fibrous surface of the bark.

Jill Powers
Buta | 2004

12 X 8 X 8 INCHES (30.5 X 20.3 X 20.3 CM)
Bark fiber, waxed linen; cooked, manipulated, cast, dyed, stitched
PHOTO © STEVE ODENDAHL

Lynn Eskridge

Cat Condo | 2004

21 X 22 X 58 INCHES
(53.3 X 55.9 X 147.3 CM)

Reed, wild cherry, leather,
black walnuts; hand dyed,
stake construction,
continuous twill construction

PHOTO © RANDY MCNEELY

Chris Ann French

Gossips | 2003

12 X 11 X 32 INCHES (30.5 X 27.9 X 81.3 CM)

Cattail, yucca, round reed; figure-eight stitch, Peruvian coil stitch, continuous coil construction

PHOTO © LEE SCHAFFERT

Gladys Sherman Ellis

Mattapoisett (Place of Rest) | 1999

9½ X 5½ X 9½ INCHES (24.1 X 14 X 24.1 CM)

Pine needles, raffia, ivory, wire; coiled, scrimshawed

PHOTO © JACK IDDON

Donna Cochran

Shell-tering I | 2004

7 X 23 X 20 INCHES (17.8 X 58.4 X 50.8 CM)

Driftwood bark, reed, jute; randed, twined

PHOTO © JANET DWYER

Doris Messick

Willow Haven | 2002

21½ X 17 X 42 INCHES (54.6 X 43.2 X 106.7 CM)

Willow, wisteria, osier dogwood; spiral random weave

PHOTOS © JEFF BAIRD

Stephen Johnson
Charity Bowl | 2003

8 X 9 INCHES (20.3 X 22.9 CM)
Paper, shoe polish; stapled, plaited

PHOTOS © DAMIAN JOHNSON

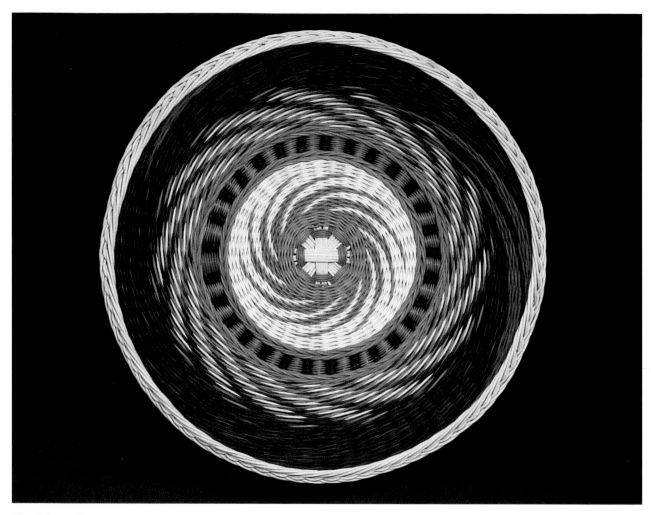

Kari Lonning

His–Hers, Spiral/Vertical | 2004

2¾ X 18½ X 18½ INCHES (7 X 47 X 47 CM)

Dyed rattan reed; five-rod wale, tapestry weaving

PHOTO © ARTIST

Francina Krayneh-Prince
Neil Prince
Carlsbad Horizon II | 2003

9 X 22 X 22 INCHES (22.9 X 55.9 X 55.9 CM)
Torrey pine needles, waxed-linen cord,
raffia; dyed, coiled construction

Deborah Valoma

Clytemnestra (undone) | 2001

6 TO 12 INCHES DIAMETER (15.2 TO 30.5 CM)
Copper wire; woven, patinated,
unwoven, wound
PHOTO © LEE FATHERREE

Deborah Valoma

Desire | 2000

25 X 25 X 12 INCHES (63.5 X 63.5 X 30.5 CM)
Paper, ink, wax; stitched
PHOTO © LEE FATHEREE

Aaron Kramer

Grub | 2002

50 X 48 X 16 INCHES (127 X 121.9 X 40.6 CM)

Recycled street-sweeper bristles, used
coffee stirrers, welded armature; woven

PHOTO © CHRISTOPHER BROOKE

Fran Reed

Circling Fern | 2004

16 X 24 X 22 INCHES (40.6 X 61 X 55.9 CM)
Halibut skin, salmon skin, gut, fern, willow; stitched

PHOTOS © CHRIS AREND

Andrea Tucker-Hody
Dressed to Remember | 2004

9 X 5 X 2½ INCHES (22.9 X 12.7 X 6.4 CM)
Dyed and bleached kozo and flax;
rhinestone embellished

PHOTO © GEORGE POST

Anna S. King
Night Bird | 2005

4¾ X 4⅛ INCHES (12 X 10.5 CM)
Nylon cord, acetate, feathers,
moss, cornhusk, bird skull,
tiny book with poem; coiled

PHOTO © SHANNON TOFT

Lise Bech

Hedgerow Cauldron | 2004

11 X 16½ INCHES (28 X 42 CM)
Willows, red and green dogwood,
heather and birch twigs; waled, randed
PHOTO © SHANNON TOFTS

Sue Boyz

Vessel One | 2000

3½ X 5 X 5½ INCHES
(8.9 X 12.7 X 14 CM)
Waxed linen, washi;
knotless netting, collaged
PHOTO © NORMAL MAKIO

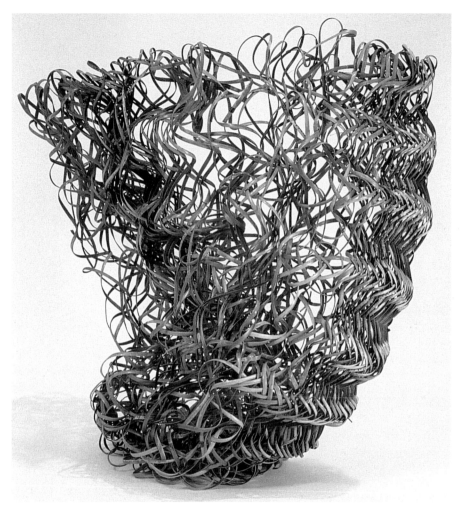

THIS PIECE *is about the changing quality of a drawn line. Some of the cane was first woven and then deconstructed to create a distorted line before it was rewoven.*

Shuna Rendel
Line Quality | 2004

17⁵⁄₁₆ X 16¹⁵⁄₁₆ X 8⅔ INCHES (44 X 43 X 22 CM)
Dyed chair cane, wire; complex linking, wrapped

PHOTOS © TAMSIN RENDEL

Betz Salmont

Untitled | 1997

18 X 8½ X 6 INCHES (45.7 X 21.6 X 15.2 CM)

Handmade paper, palm inflorescence; central form cast

THE TRANSLUCENCY *and flexibility of the materials seemed right for the vessel form and an allusion to contained space.*

Sandy Webster

Skins #17 | 2005

12 X 6 X 5 INCHES (30.5 X 15.2 X 12.7 CM)

Fabrics, sticks, thread; fused shellacked, waxed, stitched, tied

PHOTOS © ARTIST

I WANTED *to define the notion of a basket, using only the most basic suggestion of form and containment, yet not forgoing a dash of the decorative.*

Marta Herbertson

Nuts in May | 2001

11 X 22⁷⁄₁₆ INCHES (28 X 57 CM)
Eucalyptus twigs, hand-spun banana fiber, waxed linen,
acrylic paint, beeswax; tied, wrapped
PHOTOS © LLOYD HISSEY

Patricia Burleson

Dream | 2000

16 X 29 X 29 INCHES (40.6 X 73.7 X 73.7 CM)
Fabric, sticks, ballet shoe, bottle caps, keys, bones, grasses, dolls, yarns, artificial fruit, appliance cord, lace; coiled, interwoven, sewn, painted

PHOTOS © JOHN POLLACK

I AM *interested in the interplay between the found and the fabricated. Re-purposed materials retain a portion of their original entity.*

Aaron Kramer
Ice Bag, 2000

10 X 17 X 17 INCHES (25.4 X 43.2 X 43.2 CM)
Recycled street-sweeper bristles, welded armature; random weave
PHOTO © CHRISTOPHER BROOKE

Gyöngy Laky
Stain | 2000

6 X 16 X 16 INCHES
(15.2 X 40.6 X 40.6 CM)
Toothpicks, paint; glued
PHOTO © M. LEE FATHERREE

Mark Caluneo

Hive | 2003

8 X 8½ INCHES (20.3 X 21.6 CM)

Brass sheet, copper wire; hammer textured, curled, coiled, twist-tied construction technique

PHOTOS © PETER SAN CHIRICO

AS A *self-taught basket weaver with a structural-engineering background, I focus on creating unique structural basketry forms. Color combinations are achieved by using reeds that I hand dye with fiber-reactive and acid dyes. The patterns are derived to enhance the form as it develops.*

Herman Guetersloh

Rendezvous | 2005

26 X 14 INCHES (66 X 35.6 CM)
Reed, fiber-reactive and acid dyes; hand dyed, double-wall construction
PHOTO © RICK WELLS

Djupuduwuy Guyula

Dhimbuka | 2001

11 ¹³/₁₆ X 5 ⅛ INCHES (30 X 13 CM)
Hand-dyed and natural
pandanus, hand-spun kurrajong
string; twined construction

PHOTO © LOUISE HAMBY

Eva Maria Keiser

Geo Hex | 2003

3 ½ X 2 ½ X 2 ½ INCHES (8.9 X 6.4 X 6.4 CM)
Swarovski crystals, fire-polished beads, cylinder
beads, leather and vintage button; beaded,
peyote stitched, netted, embroidered

PHOTO © STEVEN RIDNOR

Anne Folehave

Round with Rubber Pieces | 2005

11 7/16 X 19 11/16 INCHES (29 X 50 CM)
Willow, rubber from bikes
PHOTO © KURT HANSEN

Virginia Kaiser

Second Skin | 2002

HEIGHT: 17⁵⁄₁₆ INCHES (44 CM)
Pine needles, pine scales;
stitched with cotton

PHOTOS © GREG PIPER

JoAnne Russo

Crab Claws | 2004

9 X 7 X 7 INCHES (22.9 X 17.8 X 17.8 CM)

Black ash, beads, pine needles, waxed linen, crab claws; woven, sewn

Krista Spieler

Green Spiral | 2003

2½ X 5¼ INCHES (6.4 X 13.3 CM)
Waxed linen, hemp-twine core, seed beads;
coiled basketry construction, stitched
PHOTO © PETER LEE

INFLUENCED BY *studies in zoology,*
I often use animal forms in my beadwork.

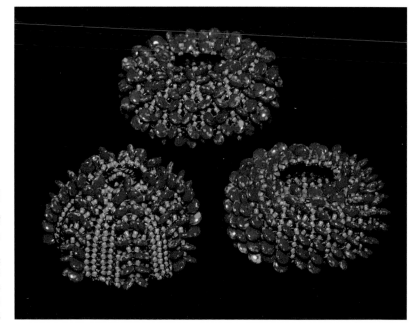

Carol Perrenoud

Herringbone Weave
Sea Urchin Trio | 2003

LEFT: 2½ X 1¼ INCHES (6.4 X 3.2 CM);
RIGHT: 2¼ X 1¾ INCHES (5.7 X 4.4 CM)

Glass seed beads, Czech pressed-glass
lentils; bead weaving, herringbone stitch

PHOTO © GARY LEE BETTS

THE VESSELS *I create are both transparent and translucent and hold secrets and mysteries. They have been evolving into a new sculptural form, one more akin to the human body—yet another container with its own mysteries inside.*

Kiyomi Iwata
Torso: Red Two | 2004

24 X 19½ X 15 INCHES (61 X 49.5 X 38.1 CM)
Dyed and stiffened silk organza, paint, wire; stitched,
embellished, embroidered French knots, fabricated

PHOTO © D. JAMES DEE

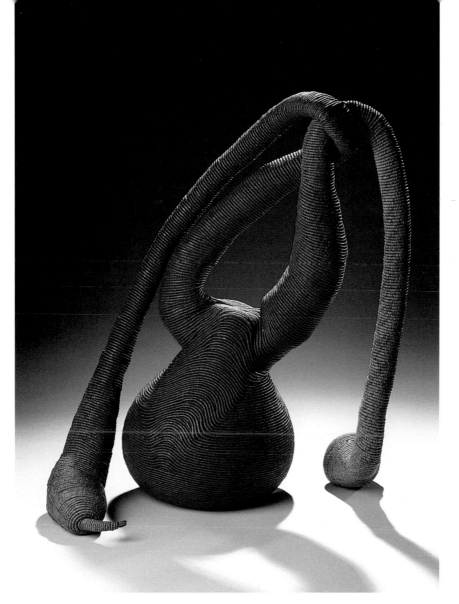

Jane Sauer

Double Vision | 2001

21 X 15 X 19 INCHES (53.3 X 38.1 X 48.3 CM)

Waxed linen, pigment

PHOTO © WENDY MCEAHERN
COURTESY DEL MANO GALLERY

Angie Harbin

Organza | 2001

13 X 5 X 8 INCHES (33 X 12.7 X 20.3 CM)

Nylon, epoxy resin, paint, wax

PHOTO © MARGO GEIST

Karyl Sisson

Moody Blue | 2003

9 X 15 X 20 INCHES (22.9 X 38.1 X 50.8 CM)

Vintage ribbon, thread, miniature
wooden spring-operated clothespins;
twined, stitched

PHOTO © SUSAN EINSTEIN

Mary Merkel-Hess

Sperry | 2003

21 X 24 X 10 INCHES (53.3 X 61 X 25.4 CM)

Reed, paper, acrylic paint, metallic watercolor, papier-mâché

PHOTO © ARTIST

Michael Davis

Textured Vessel | 2004

34 X 36 X 28 INCHES (86.4 X 91.4 X 71.1 CM)

Reed, acrylic, enamel paint, ash

THIS WALL of *purse-baskets contains small collections of some of my precious, yet mundane, worldly goods, barely visible inside woven forms, enhanced with the brilliance of fired enamels.*

Mary Chuduk

Collection Baskets | 2005

EACH: 12 X 10 X 4 INCHES (30.5 X 25.4 X 10.2 CM)

Copper wire, glass enamel, dried roses, postage stamps, shells, sea sponges, bones, seed pods, paper origami, chopsticks, clear acrylic sheet; woven, altered warp and weft, folded, gathered, sewn, enameled

PHOTO © JEFF SCOVIL

Jennifer Maestre

Aurora | 2005

7 X 17 X 17 INCHES (17.8 X 43.2 X 43.2 CM)

Pencil stubs; drilled, peyote-stitch beading

PHOTOS © DEAN POWELL

THIS BASKET *was inspired by a colorful dance during a Cinco de Mayo celebration.*

Mary Lee Fulkerson

Fiesta | 2004

14 X 24 X 24 INCHES (35.6 X 61 X 61 CM)

Willow, cable ties, paint; lashed construction

PHOTOS © SUSAN MANTLE

MY FAVORITE *letter of the alphabet is the dramatic X. Not only does its bold shape intrigue me, but also its dual meaning. If I use the letter in a work, it could mean I'm crossing out an unwanted section of the basket's wall, or I could be marking a special spot, inviting the viewer's eyes to linger where the arms of the X cross.*

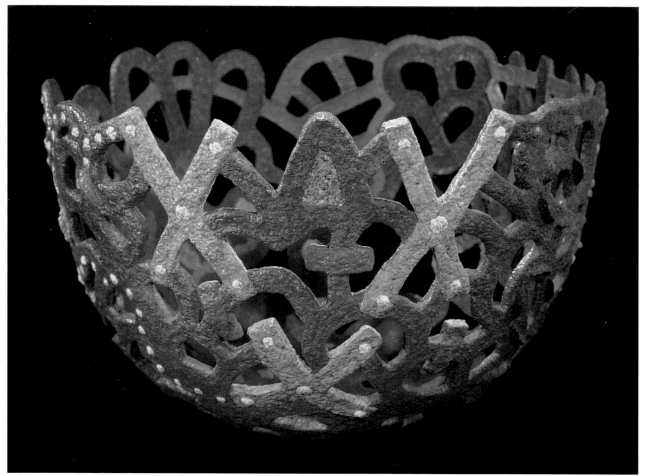

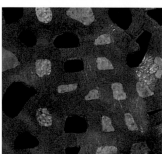

Carolyn Dahl

Flying X Basket | 2002

12 X 19 X 19 INCHES (30.5 X 48.3 X 48.3 CM)
Hand-dyed, hand-made abaca and cotton paper;
inlay technique, double- wall construction
PHOTOS © RICK WELLS

Miriam Timmons

Beauty and the Beads Basket | 2005

5 X 6 X 6 INCHES (12.7 X 15.2 X 15.2 CM)

Glass seed beads, wood beads, nylon thread, wool and nylon yarn; circular Comanche stitch, continuous construction

PHOTO © ARTIST

Barbara Schulman

Money and Pain | 2004

6½ X 10 X 5 INCHES (15.2 X 25.4 X 12.7 CM)

Hand-dyed industrial-wool felt, craft-knife blades, credit-card fragments, linen thread; hand embroidered

PHOTO © JACK RAMSDALE

THIS WORK *is intended to raise questions about the symbolic language of identification that we use to create order in our lives. It is about transforming and transformations, with the first link being the origin of the materials and the final link being the technique. Also, it is about making connections between two and three dimensions, because the piece was woven flat on the loom, then folded.*

June Kerseg-Hinson

Bolsillo De Corazon (Heart's Vessel) | 2003

14 X 8 X 5½ INCHES (35.6 X 20.3 X 14 CM)

Hand-spun kozo paper, copper magnet wire, acrylic paint, pigment, glass beads, steel wire armature; loom-warped knotted netting, interlaced, wrapped, folded

PHOTOS © BILL SMYTHE

Rosalie Friis-Ross

Promise of a Rainbow | 2001

5⅜ X 2¾ X 4 INCHES (13.9 X 7 X 10.2 CM)

Waxed linen, polystyrene foam, gesso, polyurethane

PHOTO © BERNARD WOLF
COURTESY DEL MANO GALLERY

Kate Anderson

Lichtenstein Teapot: Hopeless! | 2003

9¼ X 9¾ X 1¾ INCHES (23.5 X 24.8 X 4.4 CM)
Waxed linen, wood, silver paint; knotted

PHOTOS © TONY DECK

Kate Anderson

Warhol–Haring Teapot: Mickey Mouse | 2004

8¾ X 10¼ X 2 INCHES (22.2 X 26 X 5.1 CM)

Waxed linen, stainless steel; knotted

PHOTOS © TONY DECK

Jennifer Maestre

Asteridae | 2005

5 X 24 X 24 INCHES (12.7 X 61 X 61 CM)
Pencil stubs; drilled,
peyote-stitch beading
PHOTO © DEAN POWELL

Carole Hetzel

Brendan #84 | 2003

7½ X 22 X 22 INCHES
(19.1 X 55.9 X 55.9 CM)
Hand-dyed red reed,
stainless-steel cable;
double-woven
continuous construction
PHOTO © ALLAN CARLISLE

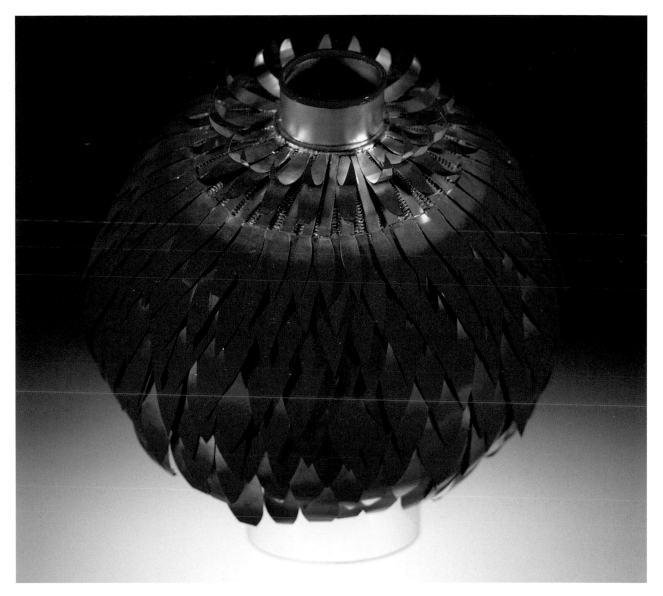

Michael Davis

A Gloaming Display | 2003

32 X 28 X 28 INCHES (81.3 X 71.1 X 71.1 CM)

Reed, enamel and acrylic paint, tin, ash

PHOTO © DELOYE BURRELL

Wayne Henderson

Heart Quiver | 2004

36 X 24 X 24 INCHES (91.4 X 61 X 61 CM)
Reed, rubber, maple stand; hand dyed
PHOTO © SETH TICE-LEWIS

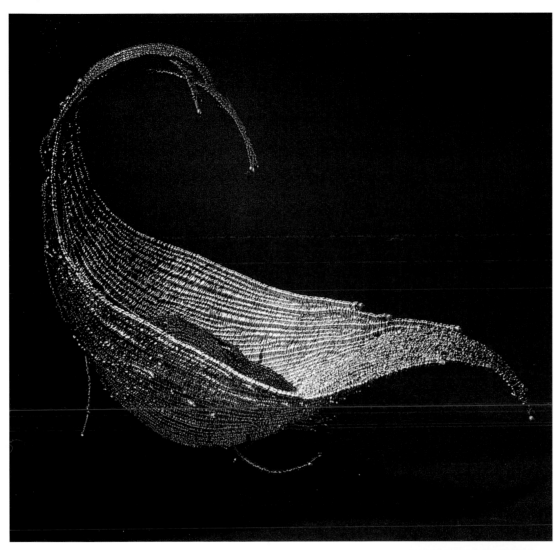

I HAD *been working with color and thought I would try something in black and silver. Once I got started, I just had to add the orange as a striking contrast to the silver and black. The piece, once finished, had a striking resemblance to a bird, thus the title* Lady of the Waters.

Marilyn Moore

Lady of the Waters | 2004

7¾ X 9½ X 4 INCHES (19.7 X 24.1 X 10.2 CM)
Polynylon-coated copper wire,
silver-plated wire over copper wire

PHOTOS © WILLIAM WICKETT

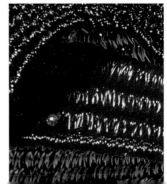

COLLECTING FOUND

objects and unwanted zippers requires patience. It can take up to a year to acquire the zippers to make a particular piece. I scour thrift stores and garage sales for zippers, having too much fun at times I admit. Friends and acquaintances find and save materials as well. Saving zippers from the landfill has become an obsession.

Susie Colquitt

Jester | 2004

7 X 6½ X 7 INCHES (17.8 X 16.5 X 17.8 CM)
Recycled metal zippers

PHOTOS © JIM ANDES

Jóh Ricci

Late Bloomer | 2004

4 X 4¼ INCHES (10.2 X 10.8 CM)
Nylon; knotted, crocheted

PHOTO © T. R. WAILLES

Susie Colquitt

Colors in Water: Michigan | 2004

5 X 6½ X 8 INCHES (12.7 X 16.5 X 20.3 CM)
Recycled nylon zippers

PHOTO © JIM ANDES

Stephen Kostyshyn

Large Jar | 2004

24 X 20 X 20 INCHES (61 X 50.8 X 50.8 CM)

Clay, reed, palm, red osier, ash; wheel
thrown, altered, assembled, woven

PHOTO © ARTIST

Priscilla Henderson

Tea | 1997

11 X 17 X 17 INCHES (27.9 X 43.2 X 43.2 CM)
Reed, hard maple, black lacquer,
loom-woven linen napkin

PHOTOS © LEE HENDERSON

John Skau

Interweave | 2003

21½ X 21½ X 6½ INCHES (54.6 X 54.6 X 16.5 CM)
Maple, cherry, paint, varnish
PHOTO © ARTIST

Joanna Gilmour

Madly Woven | 2004

14½ X 2¼ INCHES (36 X 7 CM)
Bleached paper cords, flax, willow;
hand dyed, three-directional plaited
PHOTO © ARTIST

A sculptural *basket inspired by ancient standing stones.*

John Skau

Obelisk | 2003

50 X 20 X 18 INCHES (127 X 50.8 X 45.7 CM)

Maple, paint, varnish; pattern weave, closed-end tubular form

PHOTOS © ARTIST

Elaine Small

Triple Triad | 1997

6½ X 5 X 4 INCHES (16.5 X 12.7 X 10.2 CM)

Waxed linen, polystyrene foam; knotted

PHOTOS © RED ELF

Beverly Semmens

Coalescence | 2001

21 X 19 X 7 INCHES (53.3 X 48.3 X 17.8 CM)
Raffia, jute, bamboo brushes; coiled
PHOTOS © JOHN OAKS

Aaron Yakim

Swing-Handled Egg Basket with Braid | 2004

10 X 9 X 6 INCHES (25.4 X 22.9 X 15.2 CM)

Hand-split white oak; rib-work construction,
carved, bent, pegged, whittled, woven

PHOTOS © ROBERT BATEY

JoAnne Russo

Fabergé Egg | 2005

11 X 6 X 6 INCHES (27.9 X 15.2 X 15.2 CM)

Black ash, beads, waxed linen, pine
needles; woven, sewn

PHOTO © JEFF BAIRD

> **THE PROCESS** *of gathering and preparing
> materials guides me in understanding the
> appropriate use for bark from each tree.*

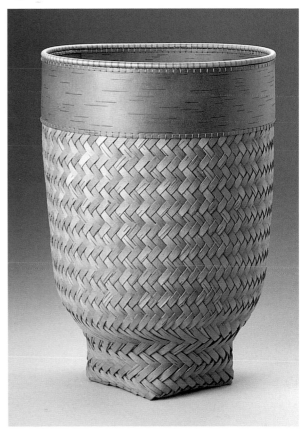

Dona Look

#2004-8 | 2004

13¼ X 9 X 9 INCHES (33.7 X 22.9 X 22.9 CM)

White birch bark, waxed silk thread;
woven, sewn, partially wrapped

PHOTO © SUSAN EINSTEIN

ALL ELEMENTS *of my baskets are created from the tree with hand tools, in the tradition of the central and southern Appalachian Mountains region.*

Aaron Yakim

Vertically Ribbed Egg Basket | 2002

11 X 13½ X 10 INCHES (27.9 X 34.3 X 25.4 CM)

Hand-split white oak; rib-work construction, pegged, wrapped

PHOTOS © JIM OSBORN

Cynthia W. Taylor

Deep Converging Ribbed Basket with Braid | 2001

14½ X 10½ X 8½ INCHES (36.8 X 26.7 X 21.6 CM)

Hand-split white oak; rib-work construction

PHOTO © JIM OSBORN

Charlotte Smith

Therapy | 1999

8 X 16 INCHES (20.3 X 40.6 CM)
Pine needles, natural raffia;
hand-coiled, stitched

PHOTO © GREG CAMPBELL

Joleen Gordon

1998-2 | 1998

$3^{15}/_{16}$ X $7^{1}/_{2}$ X $6^{11}/_{16}$ INCHES (10 X 19 X 17 CM)
Waxed and polished-linen thread; coiled
PHOTO © JULIAN BEVERIDGE

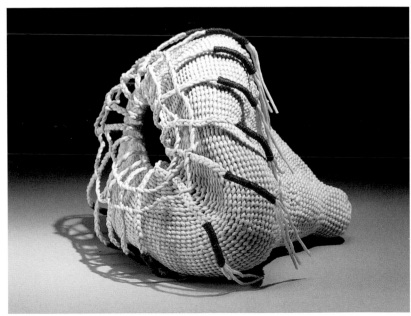

Susan Goebel Dickman

Web with Red | 2004

$4^{1}/_{2}$ X $5^{1}/_{2}$ X $5^{1}/_{2}$ INCHES (11.4 X 14 X 14 CM)
Waxed linen; twined, braided, coiled
PHOTO © PETRONELLA YTSMA

Flo Hoppe

Khamari | 2003

8 X 11½ INCHES (20.3 X 29.2 CM)

Rattan, Japanese and Malaysian cane, tiger bamboo, cedar bark; dyed, twined, embroidered, embellished

PHOTOS © JOHN C. KEYS

ONDATA *uses Japanese materials (tiger bamboo and Japanese cane) and is decorated with surface embroidery and embellishment techniques taught to me by a master Japanese basketmaker. The outer basket is woven over an older one I'd made years before and despaired of doing anything with. The solution was very satisfying.*

Flo Hoppe

Ondata | 2004

9½ INCHES DIAMETER (24.1 CM)

Rattan, Japanese and Malaysian cane, tiger bamboo; dyed, double-basket technique, twined, embroidered, embellished

PHOTO © ARTIST

Martha Van Meter

Old Fish | 2003

1 X 10 X ¾ INCHES (2.5 X 25.4 X 1.9 CM)

Pine needles, fossil set in resin, coils, faux sinew; dyed, sewn

PHOTO © ARTIST

Maggie Tetreault

Simply Symmetry | 2003

5½ X 8 X 8 INCHES (14 X 20.3 X 20.3 CM)

Long-leaf pine needles, raffia, gourd; coil construction

PHOTO © JEFF BAIRD

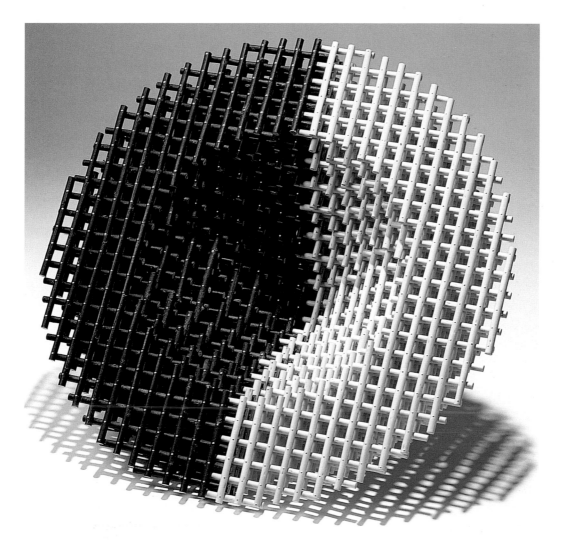

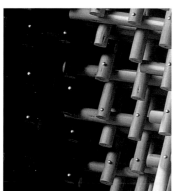

Dail Behennah

Black and White Willow Bowl | 2004

10¹³⁄₁₆ X 25⁹⁄₁₆ X 25⁹⁄₁₆ INCHES (27.5 X 65 X 65 CM)

Black and white willow, white willow,
silver-plated pins; drilled, constructed

PHOTOS © JASON INGRAM

Dorothy Gil Barnes

Seven Moons | 1995

16 X 11 INCHES DIAMETER (40.6 X 27.9 CM)
Pine, dendroglyph

PHOTO © DOUG MARTIIN
COURTESY DEL MANO GALLERY

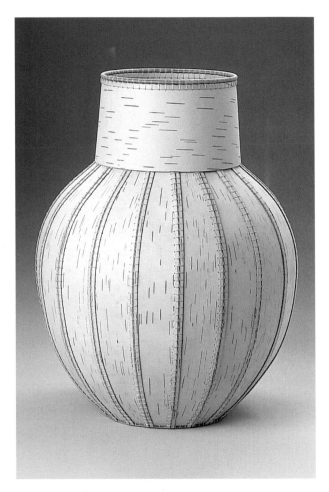

Dona Look

#2004–2 | 2004

13 X 10 X 10 INCHES (33 X 25.4 X 25.4 CM)
White birch bark, waxed silk thread; sewn,
partially wrapped

PHOTO © SUSAN EINSTEIN

Helen Frost Way

Story Basket II | 2004

17 X 11 INCHES (43.2 X 27.9 CM)

Cotton fiber; coiled, collaged, painted

PHOTOS © RON MCCOY

THE JAPANESE *samurai warrior's helmet, the* kawari-kabuto, *more than protects the head; it also serves as a mask—a disguise that transforms the wearer— and makes him larger than life. These very distinctive helmets, with their attached sculptural forms, are examples of individual self–expression not commonly found in Japanese culture. In my kawari-kabuto pieces, one can see the influences of my American-Japanese ancestry, materials from my Hawaii home, and my love for basketmaking.*

Gail M. Toma

Helmet with Goat Skull and Horns II | 2001

27 X 24 X 22 INCHES (68.6 X 61 X 55.9 CM)

Hand-dyed round reed and abaca fiber, goat skull from Hawaii, 22-karat gold leaf, Japanese handmade paper, paint; chase weave

PHOTO © BRIAN SATO

Gail M. Toma

Helmet | 1998

22 X 16 X 18 INCHES (55.9 X 40.6 X 45.7 CM)

Round reed, hand-dyed round reed, areca, McArthur and
princess palm inflorescence, upholstery tacks, gourd
pieces, synthetic gold leaf, hemp fiber; chase weave

PHOTO © BRIAN SATO

JoAnne Russo

Harlequin in a Tutu | 2004

9 X 10 X 10 INCHES (22.9 X 25.4 X 25.4 CM)
Black ash, pine needles, waxed linen,
fish vertebrae; woven

PHOTOS © JEFF BAIRD

Lindsay Ketterer Rais

Split in Two | 2003

25 X 24 X 9 INCHES
(63.5 X 61 X 22.9 CM)

Stainless-steel mesh,
pistachio shells, silver wire,
beads, steel; pleated, stitched,
knotless netting

PHOTO © D. JAMES DEE

Lois Russell

Almost Spring | 2004

3 X 4 X 4 INCHES
(7.6 X 10.2 X 10.2 CM)
Waxed linen, thread

PHOTO © JEFF MAGIDSON

Ruth Greenberg

Dragon | 1998

1 ¾ X 2 ½ X 1 ¾ INCHES (4.4 X 6.4 X 4.4 CM)
Bindweed, driftwood

PHOTO © DAVID PETERS
COURTESY DEL MANO GALLERY

Cynthia W. Taylor

Shallow Hen Basket with Converging Ribbing and Braid | 2004

9½ X 10 X 7 INCHES (24.1 X 25.4 X 17.8 CM)

Hand-split white oak; carved, whittled, rib-work construction

PHOTOS © ROBERT BATEY

FULLY FUNCTIONAL, *the zippers are from my Dad's collection of stuff—no clue as to what he was going to do with them. By using various sizes in a regular pattern, a natural curve occurred, allowing the zipper ends to pull up through the center.*

Judy A. Dominic

For the Giving | 2004

6 X 10 INCHES (15.2 X 25.4 CM)

Zippers, thread, beads; machine and hand sewn

PHOTOS © CINDY WAGNER

Christine Love Adcock

Bear Claw Basket | 2005

13 X 8 INCHES (33 X 20.3 CM)

Dyed date-palm inflorescence, Colter
pine-cone scales; woven, coiled

PHOTO © MEHOSH DZIADZIO

MY WORK *is often environmentalist in nature and inspiration. Both the cactus form and the garden hose are strong water symbols, speaking to both conservation and consumption. If you look at the inside bottom of the basket, you'll see I used a drain for the center start. The valve handles used for flowers represent the choices we make everyday that affect our water conserva-tion and consumption.*

Brian Jewett

Choices | 2004

62 X 20 X 20 INCHES (157.5 X 50.8 X 50.8 CM)
Garden hose, cable ties, valve handles;
coiled construction

PHOTOS © BRIAN FORREST

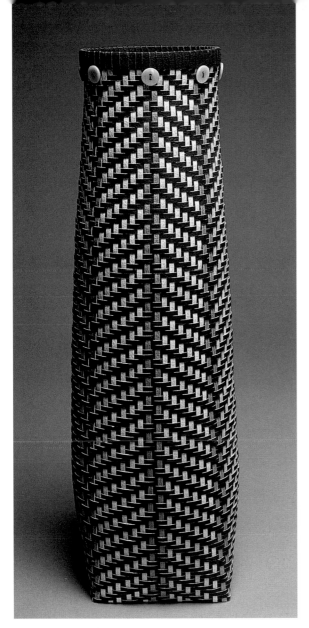

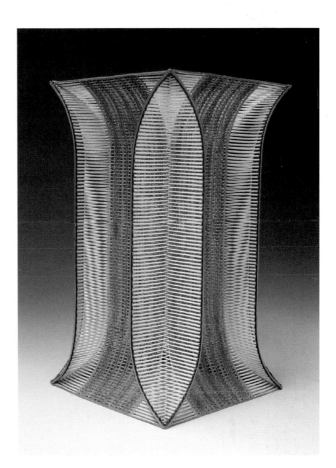

Dennis Nahabetian

Vessel #65 | 2004

7¾ X 3¼ X 3¼ INCHES (19.7 X 9.5 X 9.5 CM)

Copper, bronze, patina with polychrome; metalsmithing and textile techniques

PHOTO © ARTIST

Mary M. Miller

Tower | 2004

17 X 6 X 6 INCHES (43.2 X 15.2 X 15.2 CM)

Paper, paint, waxed linen, buttons; plaited

PHOTO © STEPHEN PETEGORSKY

Amy O'Connell

Spider Basket | 2004

4 X 7 X 7 INCHES (10.2 X 17.8 X 17.8 CM)
Copper wire; fabricated
PHOTO © ARTIST

Biba Schutz

Basket with Curls | 2001

6 X 9½ X 8 INCHES (15.2 X 24.1 X 20.3 CM)
Steel, copper, bronze, wire;
constructed frame wrapped with
forged and beaded wires

PHOTO © RON BOSZKO

AS I weave, I build an asymmetrical shape that gives the basket a front that faces the viewer, often with a forward lean and graceful lines. I think of my baskets as having postures as they stand erect. These qualities are subtle, and the work remains a vessel.

Leon Niehues
#22-04 | 2004

30 X 14 X 14 INCHES (76.2 X 35.6 X 35.6 CM)
Dyed and natural local white oak, coral-berry runners, waxed-linen thread; split, woven free-form, drilled, stitched
PHOTO © SEAN MOORMAN

Judy Mulford
By the Sea | 2001

12 X 12 INCHES (30.5 X 30.5 CM)
Gourds, waxed linen, beach sand, photo transfers, polymer clay, antique buttons, pearls, pounded tin-can lids, spoons, fine silver; knotted, looped

PHOTOS © SUSAN EINSTEIN

Laura Balombini

In the Garden House, Friends Gather to Tell Stories | 2004

18 X 10 X 10 INCHES (45.7 X 25.4 X 25.4 CM)

Steel wire, polymer clay; hand woven, attached figures

PHOTO © ARTIST

139

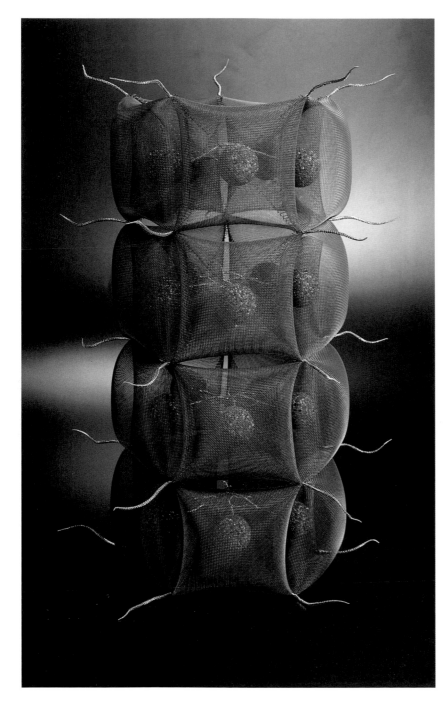

Lanny Bergner

Space Container | 2004

28 X 19 X 19 INCHES (71.1 X 48.3 X 48.3 CM)

Charcoal aluminum screen, glass frit, wire;
hand connected, glued, wrapped

PHOTO © WILLIAM WICKETT

Nancy Koenigsberg

Double Pleat | 2004

13 X 16 X 10 INCHES (33 X 40.6 X 25.4 CM)

Polynylon-coated copper wire, annealed steel wire, knotted strips; sewn, folded

PHOTO © D. JAMES DEE

Briana-Lyn Syvarth

End Over End | 2001

38 X 16 X 10 INCHES (96.5 X 40.6 X 25.4 CM)

Steel wire; tinkering technique

PHOTO © D. JAMES DEE

I AM *extremely interested in architecture, and buildings influence many of my works. In this case, the piece is more literal than most.*

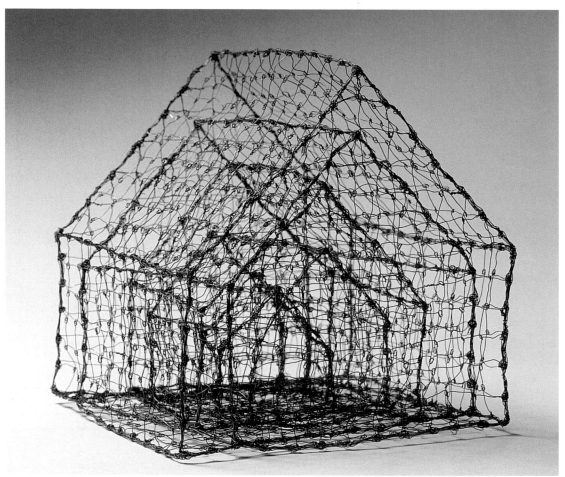

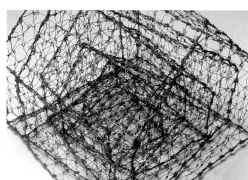

Nancy Koenigsberg

Concentric Houses | 2001

10½ X 10½ X 10½ INCHES (26.7 X 26.7 X 26.7 CM)

Annealed steel wire; woven sections using modified soumak technique, sewn

PHOTOS © D. JAMES DEE

John McQueen

Turning My World on Its Ear | 2005

61 X 38 X 28 INCHES (154.9 X 96.5 X 71.1 CM)

Bark, sticks, string

PHOTO © ARTIST
COURTESY OF DEL MANO GALLERY

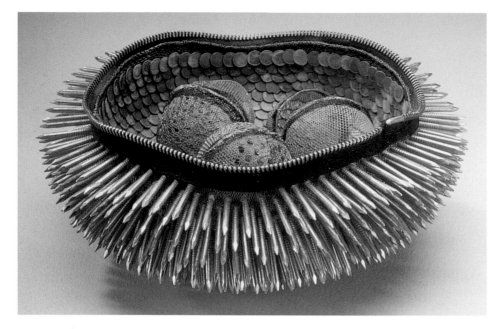

Jennifer Maestre

Dreaming | 2000

4½ X 9 X 9 INCHES (11.4 X 22.9 X 22.9 CM)
Copper nails, copper screen, zippers;
nails pushed through screen, sewn

PHOTO © DEAN POWELL

Minna Koskinen

Hyrrä | 2002

9⅞ INCHES DIAMETER (25 CM)
Wire, willow; plait, spiral technique

PHOTO © ARTIST

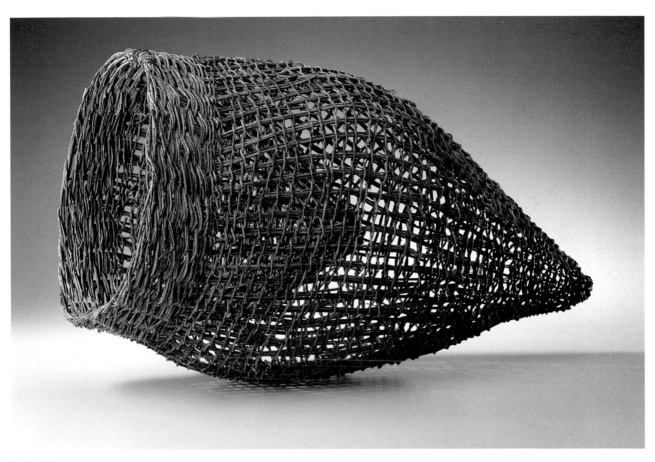

Julia Parker

Fish Trap | 2002

12 X 12 X 24 INCHES (30.5 X 30.5 X 61 CM)

Willow; windowpane twining

Jeanine Phifer Howell

Tall Basket | 2002

22½ X 7 X 5 INCHES (57.2 X 17.8 X 12.7 CM)
Stoneware, stains, clear glaze; hand built, press molded, rolled, woven

PHOTOS © J. SCHMUKI

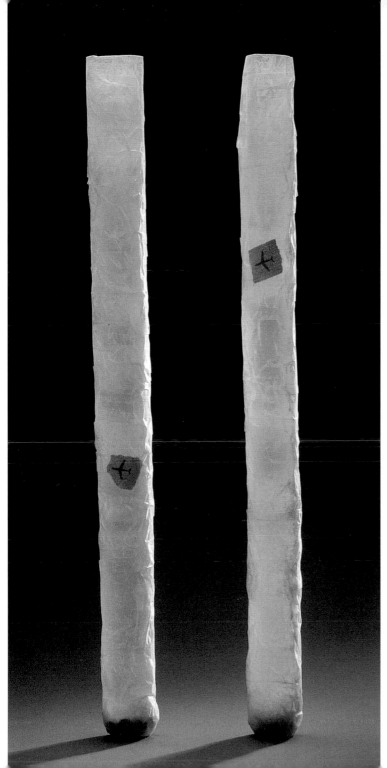

Bird Ross

Par Avion | 2001

30 X 2 X 2 INCHES (76.2 X 5.1 X 5.1 CM)

Tape, pennies, paper-envelope pieces; constructed

PHOTOS © TOM MCINVAILLE

THE MANY *pulsing rhythms of nature provide a grid or substrate for metaphysical flight. Here, the juxtaposition of wing beats and drumbeats creates a visual resonance.*

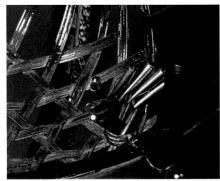

Penelope Sharp

Winged Drumbeats | 2005

40 X 15 X 15 INCHES (101.6 X 38.1 X 38.1 CM)
Rattan, ash, bamboo, copper, Swarovski crystals, Lady Amherst pheasant feathers, brass screws; woven, lacquered, formed, stitched
PHOTOS © KEN SANVILLE

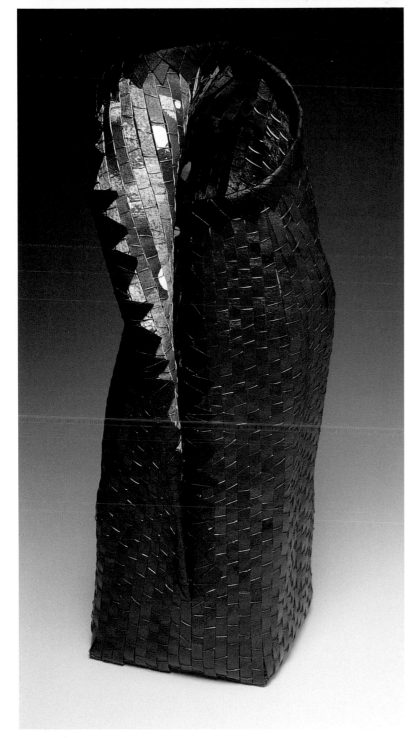

Jackie Abrams
Looking Out | 2004

15 X 5 X 5 INCHES (38.1 X 12.7 X 12.7 CM)
Cotton paper, paint, waxed linen,
varnish; woven

PHOTOS © JEFF BAIRD

Betz Salmont

Sedona | 1995

18 X 8 X 8½ INCHES (45.7 X 20.3 X 21.6 CM)
Handmade paper with eucalyptus pods and
dracaena leaves; cast paper, woven central basket
PHOTO © ARTIST

Sandy Webster

Skins #18 | 2005

10 X 6 X 5 INCHES (25.4 X 15.2 X 12.7 CM)
Fabrics, sticks, thread; fused,
shellacked, waxed, stitched, tied
PHOTO © ARTIST

Pat Hickman

Doubled: Death Be Not Proud | 1995

27 X 38 X 35 INCHES (68.6 X 96.5 X 88.9 CM)

Gut, pandanus, reed, sennit, acrylic, colored ink

PHOTOS © BRAD GODA
COURTESY DEL MANO GALLERY

Jan Buckman

Guardian II | 2002

27 X 6 X 5 INCHES (68.6 X 15.2 X 12.7 CM)

Waxed linen, hawthorn branches; twined

PHOTOS © PETER LEE

Polly Jacobs Giacchina

Lair | 2004

36 X 11 X 8 INCHES (91.4 X 27.9 X 20.3 CM)

Date willow, washi paper, bark; twined, collaged assemblage

PHOTOS © RODNEY NAKAMOTO

Linda G. Lugenbill

Intertwined | 2002

13 X 10 X 10 INCHES (33 X 25.4 X 25.4 CM)

Reed, dyes, vines, roots, bark, waxed linen, microwood; plaited, handshaped, stitched

PHOTO © AZAD

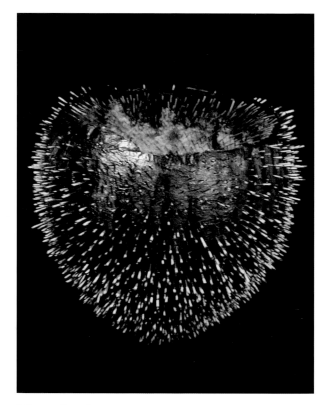

Diane Banks

Beauty Is in the Eye of the Beholder | 2003

12 X 17 INCHES (30.5 X 43.2 CM)

Rice paper, wood, dye

PHOTO © ARTIST

MUCH OF *the material used in this piece was metal I collected in the desert. Time and target practice had turned discarded appliances into beautiful art material.*

John G. Garrett

Grande | 2004

24 X 24 X 24 INCHES (61 X 61 X 61 CM)
Copper, steel, hardware cloth, wire, beads;
personal techniques

PHOTOS © MARGO GEIST

Liz Stoehr

Black Container #3 | 2002

11 X 12 X 29 INCHES (27.9 X 30.5 X 73.7 CM)
Braided elastic, thread; plain woven, stitched
PHOTO © BOB ELBERT

EACH OF *the* Saeculum *structures marks a particular lunar sequence and cumulatively compromises the progression of life.*

Donna L. Lish

Saeculum: Tunnel | 2005

15 X 11 X 11 INCHES (38.1 X 27.9 X 27.9 CM)
Aluminum, synthetics, steel; crocheted, knitted, stitched

PHOTOS © ARTIST

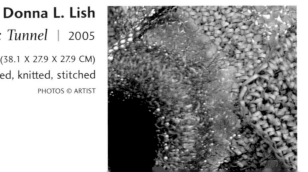

THIS IS *from my "Women Forms" series. Each form contains the shape of a woman's life—a collection of her experiences, her passions and grief, her pains and joys. Here, Sylvia is dressed up, ready for the ball.*

Jackie Abrams
Sylvia Goes to the Ball | 2005

15 X 7 X 7 INCHES (38.1 X 17.8 X 17.8 CM)
Paper, fabric, paint, wire, beads; woven
PHOTO © JEFF BAIRD

Marion Hildebrandt

Untitled | 2004

7 X 3 INCHES DIAMETER (17.8 X 7.6 CM)

Black paper twine, waxed-linen twine, black leather lava rock, white coral stone; loom woven, loop stitched

PHOTOS © HAP SAKWA
COURTESY DEL MANO GALLERY

I CREATE *the familiar teapot form as a container to hold images of visual art icons. Quotation, allusion, abstraction, and high-art/low-art references come into play as the repetitive knotting process simultaneously forms a structure, surface, and image.*

Kate Anderson

O' Keeffe Teapot: Red Poppy–White Flower | 2002

7½ X 11¼ X 2 INCHES (19.1 X 28.6 X 5.1 CM)

Waxed linen, wood; knotted

PHOTOS © TONY DECK

Linda Fifield
Kentucky WILD Flower VII | 2004

6½ X 2¾ X 2¾ INCHES (16.5 X 7 X 7 CM)
Czech glass beads, nylon thread, wood form,
netting; stitched
PHOTO © JACK FIFIELD

Cindy Wrobel
Untitled | 2005

7¼ X 6½ X 6½ INCHES (18.4 X 16.5 X 16.5 CM)
Beads, wire; strung, wrapped
PHOTO © JIM SOKOLIK

Mary Merkel-Hess

Linby | 2003

25 X 19 X 11 INCHES
(63.5 X 48.3 X 27.9 CM)
Reed, paper, acrylic paint,
papier-mâché

PHOTO © ARTIST

Suzy Wahl

Whose Rainbow Are We Chasing? | 1996

6½ X 4½ INCHES (16.5 X 11.4 CM)
Glass beads; netted beading

PHOTOS © ARTIST

David Nittmann

*Three Old Ladies and
a Little Boy* | 2004

17 X 3 INCHES (43.2 X 7.6 CM)

American holly; turned,
burned, dyed

PHOTOS © BENKO PHOTOGRAPHICS

Marilyn Moore

Sway | 2004

8½ X 5 X 4 INCHES (21.6 X 12.7 X 10.2 CM)

Polynylon-coated copper wire over copper
wire; two-strand twining construction

PHOTO © ROBERT VINNEDGE

Daniel Evan Schwartz

Struggle | 2004

6½ X 6 X 3 INCHES (16.5 X 15.2 X 7.6 CM)

Waxed-linen thread, fiber rush core; coiled, stitched

PHOTO © MICHAEL CAVANAGH

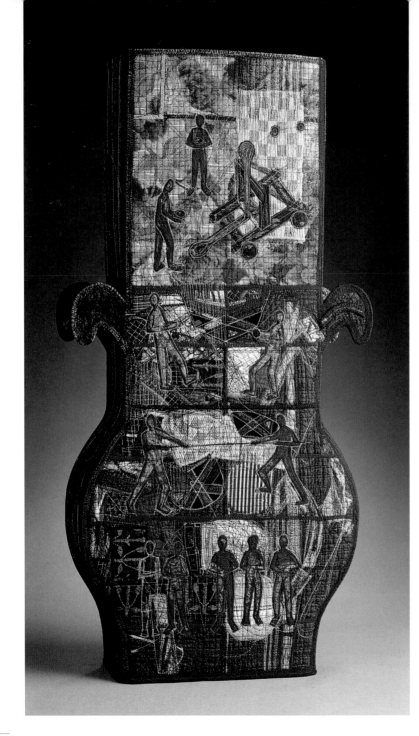

THE FOLLY *was inspired partially by the ancient Greek amphora, particularly by the horizontal bands of figures moving across the surface. On one side of this vessel, the figures are engaged in firing a catapult, and on the other side, they are building a wall.*

Kay Kahn
The Folly | 2005

36¼ X 18 X 6½ INCHES (92.1 X 45.7 X 16.5 CM)
Cotton, silk; quilted, pieced, appliquéd, hand and machine stitched, constructed
PHOTO © WENDY MCEAHERN

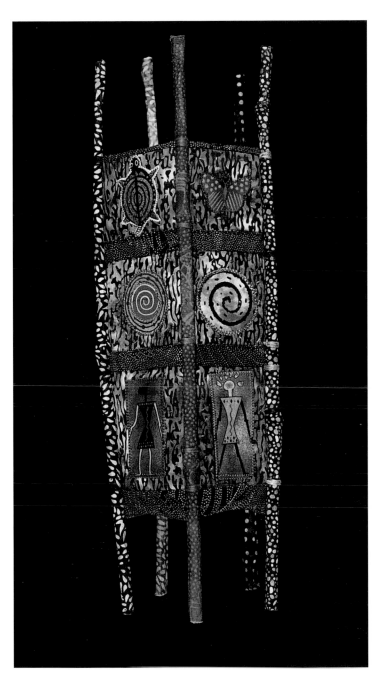

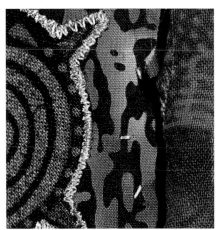

Lynne Sward

Personal Symbol Series #5 | 2005

15 X 4½ X 5½ INCHES (38.1 X 11.4 X 14 CM)
Fabric, yarn, bamboo; machine and hand sewn
PHOTOS © LEE FISHBECK

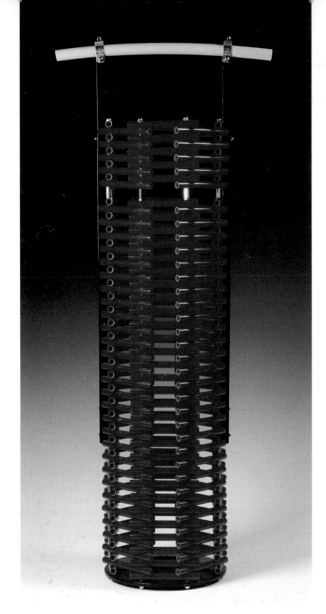

Rob Dobson

Basket # 130 | 2003

50 X 20 X 12 INCHES (127 X 50.8 X 30.5 CM)
Recycled plastic tubing, gas pipe, threaded steel rods,
wood from cable spool, pipe hangers, nuts; constructed

PHOTO © JEFF BAIRD

Elizabeth Whyte Schulze

China Lake | 2004

45 X 6½ X 3½ INCHES (114.3 X 16.5 X 8.9 CM)
Pine needles, raffia, acrylic paint; coiled

PHOTO © JOHN POLAK

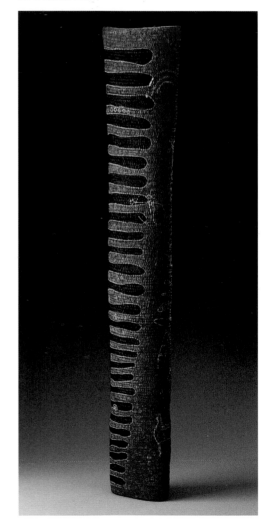

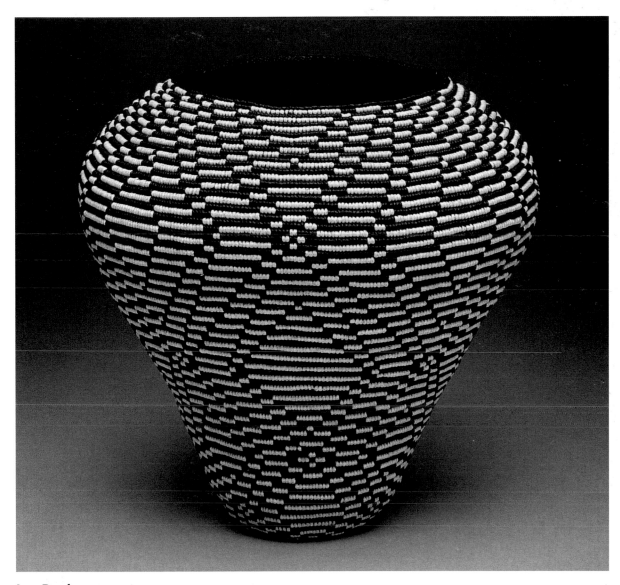

Jan Buckman

Untitled #4-05 | 2005

10¾ X 10½ INCHES (27.3 X 26.7 CM)

Waxed linen; twined

PHOTO © PETER LEE

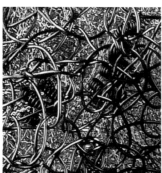

June Kerseg-Hinson

Interior Realm II | 2005

12 X 12 X 12 INCHES (30.5 X 30.5 X 30.5 CM)

Copper magnet wire, enameled copper wire, brass wire, acrylic paint, pigment; random weave, continuous construction, coiled

PHOTOS © MIKE RYAN

Dawn Walden

First People | 2001

20 X 12 X 12 INCHES (50.8 X 30.5 X 30.5 CM)
Cedar bark and roots; interlaced
PHOTO © JERRY MCGUIRE

AFTER MANY *years of faithfully weaving lovely Shaker baskets, I am now inspired to design and execute graceful, elegant vessels with a strong visual statement. My Shaker roots are evident in these baskets; indeed, those superb roots may always show.*

Sharon Dugan

Urchin | 2004

5½ X 5½ INCHES (14 X 14 CM)
Natural and dyed, pounded black-ash splint,
birch rims; continuous weave construction

PHOTO © Z. IAN RAYMOND

Tika Tucker

Aztec Sunset | 2005

9 X 23½ INCHES (22.9 X 59.7 CM)

Hand-dyed reed, quatrefoil pattern on base;
twilled, continuous weave construction

PHOTO © TIM BARNWELL

Tressa Sularz

Passages | 2004

6 X 6 X 25½ INCHES (15.2 X 15.2 X 64.8 CM)

Natural and hand-dyed rattan; reverse-twill weave

PHOTO © PETER LEE

Mary M. Miller

Waves II | 2004

5 X 17 X 5 INCHES (12.7 X 43.2 X 12.7 CM)

Paper, paint, waxed linen; plaited

PHOTO © STEPHEN PETEGORSKY

THIS WORK *resulted from a North Carolina Individual Visual Artist fellowship to explore chaos theory and fractals. The Archimedes and logarithmic spirals create fractals. If you look deeply enough into chaos, you will find order. Chaos examines unstable aperiodic (or non-repeating) behavior in nonlinear dynamical systems.*

Billie Ruth Sudduth

Fibonacci in Chaos | 2005

15 X 16 X 16 INCHES (38.1 X 40.6 X 40.6 CM)
European-cut reed splints, hand-dyed iron oxide, crushed walnut, herringbone base; twill-woven construction

PHOTO © JOHN LITTLETON

THE PATTERN *and design were created from memories I have of a dotted Swiss dress my mother made me when I was a child.*

Billie Ruth Sudduth

Shaker Wall Basket, 2004

11 X 12 X 7 INCHES (27.9 X 30.5 X 17.8 CM)

European-cut reed splints, split oak, henna and madder dyes, acrylic paint; plaited construction

PHOTO © PAUL JEREMIAS

I LIVED *on the island of Tortola in the British Virgin Islands for three years. During that time I spent hundreds of magical hours on and under the enchanting Caribbean Sea. While designing this piece, I immersed myself in memories of the sea, the extraordinary creatures within. I visualized the moving sea and flashes of brilliantly colored schools of fish. I hope that the joy I experienced is conveyed in this piece.*

Jeanie Pratt

Tortola | 2004

11 X 10 X 11 INCHES (27.9 X 25.4 X 27.9 CM)

Copper wire, seed beads, semi-precious stones, walnut; twill and supplementary-weft brocade construction

PHOTO © DALE RED
COURTESY OF THIRTEEN MOONS GALLERY

Marc Jenesel
Karen E. Pierce
Cross Currents | 2004

36 X 20 INCHES (91.4 X 50.8 CM)
Raku-fired pottery, rattan, copper wire, palm inflorescence, copper beads, waxed linen; interlaced, attached, thrown, altered

PHOTOS © MARC JENESEL

Michele Hament

Untitled | 2000

15 X 9 X 3½ INCHES (38.1 X 22.9 X 8.9 CM)

Willow, dyed reed, telephone wire, paint; twined, lashed, woven, wrapped

PHOTO © ARTIST

Barbara Trout

Sun Bands | 2005

10 X 5½ INCHES (25.4 X 14 CM)

Waxed linen, hand-dyed abaca fiber; knotted and coiled on metal frame

PHOTO © ROGER BRAHN

ILLUSIONS LOST *was a reaction to the events of September 11, 2001.*

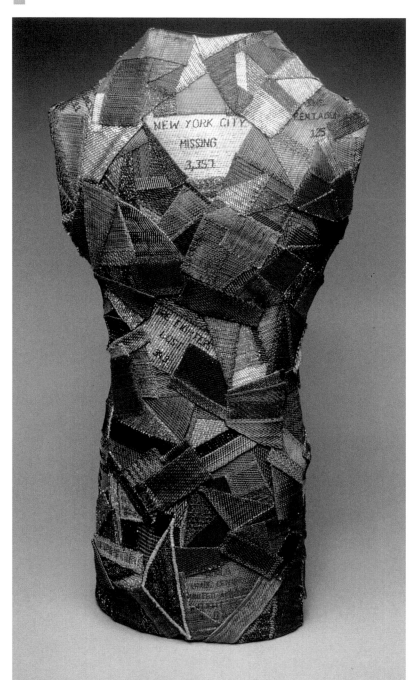

Donna Kaplan

Illusions Lost | 2002

31 X 17 X 9 INCHES (78.7 X 43.2 X 22.9 CM)
Wire, rayon, silk, linen, cotton thread; loom woven, machine and hand embroidered, machine and hand sewn

PHOTOS © JERRY MCCOLLUM

CREATED AFTER *9/11*, Taliswoman *is a vessel for protection.*

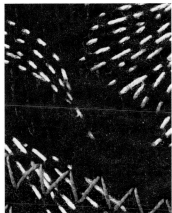

Barbara Schulman

Taliswoman | 2001

17 X 13 X 10 INCHES (43.2 X 33 X 25.4 CM)

Industrial-wool felt, cotton thread; dyed, pieced, hand embroidered

PHOTOS © ROBERT WALCH

Herman Guetersloh

Double Happiness | 2005

35 X 13 X 7 INCHES (88.9 X 33 X 17.8 CM)

Reed, fiber-reactive and acid dyes;
hand dyed, double-wall construction

PHOTO © RICK WELLS

THERE IS *text inside each animal. For the tortoise: "Better to try, and risk failing than never to try and never win." For the hare: "Keep your focus on success."*

Leah Danberg

The Tortoise and the Hare | 2004–2005

4¼ X 10¼ X 6 INCHES (11.4 X 25.4 X 15.2 CM)
AND 12 X 8 X 5½ INCHES (30.5 X 20.3 X 14 CM)

Waxed linen, cotton, polystyrene foam; knotted

PHOTOS © BERNARD WOLF

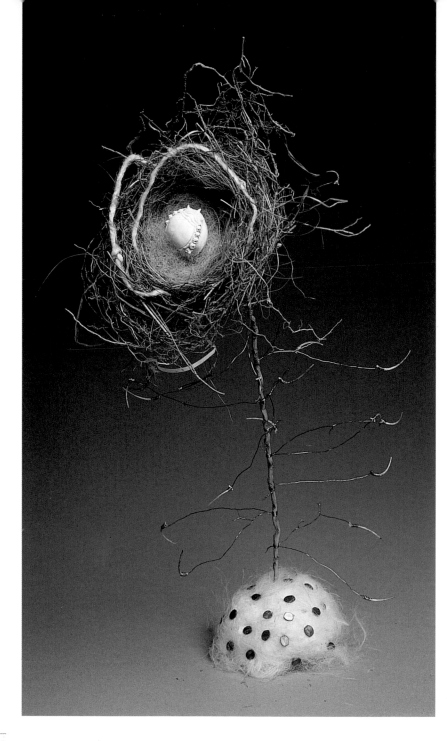

Marcella Anna Stasa

Fear to Be Contained | 2005

10 X 11 X 6 INCHES (25.4 X 27.9 X 15.2 CM)

Nest, palm stalk, copper wire, snake bones, crab shell, porcelain, carpet tacks, wool; assembled

PHOTO © DAVID CARAS

Carol Eckert

Mayan Chronicles | 2004

12½ X 16 X 3 INCHES (31.8 X 40.6 X 7.6 CM)

Cotton over wire; coiled

PHOTO © W. SCOTT MITCHELL

Gerri Johnson-McMillin

Paradise | 2005

4½ X 6 X 6 INCHES (11.4 X 15.2 X 15.2 CM)
Albacore fishbone, monofilament, glass beads;
double-basket woven

PHOTOS © ARTIST

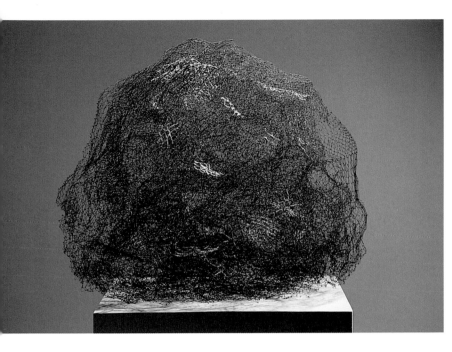

Pat Hickman
Tumbleweed | 2004

4 X 3 X 3 FEET (13.4 X 11.6 X 11.6 M)
Wire, gut (hog casings)
PHOTO © BRAD GODA
COURTESY DEL MANO GALLERY

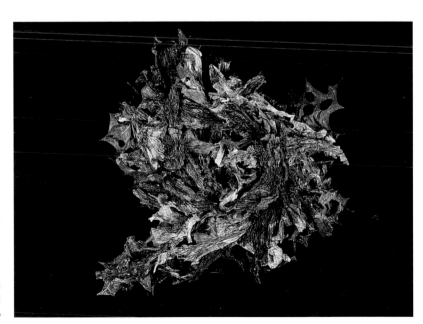

Jacy Diggins
Nest | 2004

17 X 6 INCHES (43.2 X 15.2 CM)

Waxed paper, gut, indigo, rust, thread;
pleated, pierced, dyed, rusted, tied

PHOTO © LAUREL HUNGERFORD

WHAT CAN *we control? What is beyond our control?*
My work exists at the intersection of these questions.

Kay Stanfield
Ochre Form #2 | 2002

26⅜ X 17⁵⁄₁₆ X 11¹³⁄₁₆ INCHES (67 X 44 X 30 CM)
Handmade-paper sheets of beaten linen
rag, cotton rag, raw flax, abaca, inclusions
of clothing that couldn't be beaten
(heavy seams, zippers, buttons, pockets),
clear oil stick, ochre pigment
PHOTOS © GARY CASTLE

Angie Harbin

Phoenix | 2004

9 X 28 X 9 INCHES (22.9 X 71.1 X 22.9 CM)

Nylon, epoxy resin, paint, wax

PHOTO © MARGO GEIST

John McGuire

Kernal | 2000

12 X 10 INCHES DIAMETER (30.5 X 25.4 CM)

Black ash, calabash gourd

PHOTOS © DAVID PETERS
COURTESY DEL MANO GALLERY

THIS PIECE *is from a series entitled "Fruits of My Labor." The pear is a metaphor for the female figure, and the architectural frame around the pear suggests home and safety. The work is about children and family.*

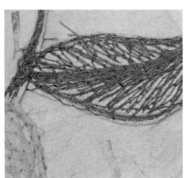

Jo Stealey

Fruits of My Labor: Fertility | 2003

15 X 9 X 2½ INCHES (38.1 X 22.9 X 6.4 CM)

Waxed linen, reed, handmade paper, paper rush, thread, silkworm cocoon; coiled, machine stitched

PHOTOS © PETER ANGER

Lissa Hunter

Mute Beauty | 2004

15 X 28 X 5 INCHES (38.1 X 71.1 X 12.7 CM)

Paper cord, waxed linen, paper, wood, drywall
compound, paint, pencil; coiled, painted, drawn

PHOTO © K. B. PILCHER
COURTESY DEL MANO GALLERY

EARLY IN *2004, I delivered a paper in New Delhi, India.*
The colors of the textiles and buildings took my breath away!

Nancy Moore Bess

Five Shades of Red | 2004

5 X 16 X 5 INCHES (12.7 X 40.6 X 12.7 CM)

Wooden Japanese box, waxed cotton and linen,
wooden Indian lids, beads, Chinese lacquer,
joss papers; twined, knotted

PHOTOS © D. JAMES DEE

Leslee Ann Burtt

Deer Basket | 2002

24 X 24 X 18 INCHES (61 X 61 X 45.7 CM)

Mule-deer antler, seagrass, reed, cedar bark; ribbed

PHOTO © BILL BACHHUBER

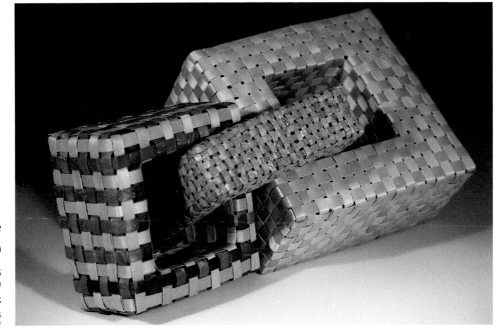

John McGuire

Chain Reaction | 2000

14 X 10 X 14 INCHES
(35. 6 X 25.4 X 35. 6 CM)
Red cedar, black oak

PHOTO © DAVID PETERS
COURTESY DEL MANO GALLERY

Joanna E. Schanz

Embellished Round #1 | 2005

9 X 13 X 13 INCHES (22.9 X 33 X 33 CM)
Peeled and unpeeled willow; twined,
double twined

PHOTO © ARTIST

John McQueen

Manhandled | 2004

34 X 19 X 8½ INCHES (86.4 X 48.3 X 21.6 CM)

Sticks, bark, hot glue

PHOTO © ARTIST
COURTESY OF DEL MANO GALLERY

Priscilla Henderson

Pedestal Bowl | 1987

21 X 15 INCHES (53.3 X 38.1 CM)

Reed, hard maple, black lacquer; frisketed, airbrushed

PHOTO © LEE HENDERSON

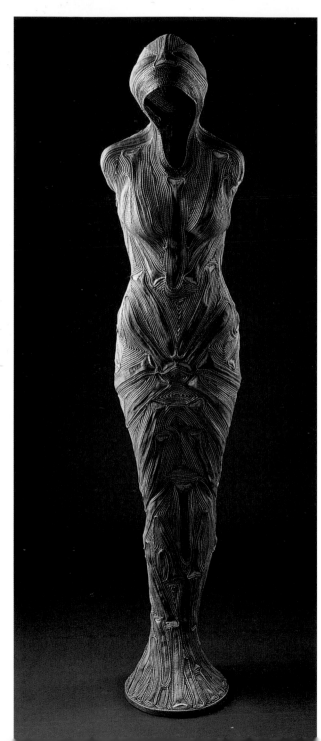

Jan Hopkins

Contemplation | 2004

72 X 14 X 12 INCHES (182.9 X 35.6 X 30.5 CM)

Agave leaves, yellow-cedar bark, waxed linen; stitched, molded, coiled with a looping technique

PHOTOS © WENDY MCEAHERN

Beverly Semmens

Child Basket II | 2000

14 X 7 X 5 INCHES (35.6 X 17.8 X 12.7 CM)

Linen, antique shoes; crocheted

PHOTO © JOHN OAKS

Ann Hall Richards

Out Growth | 2002

26 X 7 X 5 INCHES (66 X 17.8 X 12.7 CM)

Cast paper, twined waxed linen

PHOTO © WENDY MCEAHERN
COURTESY DEL MANO GALLERY

I **HAVE** taken poetic license with a knight's armor and current concerns about body armor by designing a mock metal protector.

Dona Anderson
Knight's Armor #IV | 2005

30 X 25 X 5 INCHES (76.2 X 63.5 X 12.7 CM)
Round and flat reed, polymer emulsion, paint, nuts, bolts, washers
PHOTO © ROB VINNEDGE

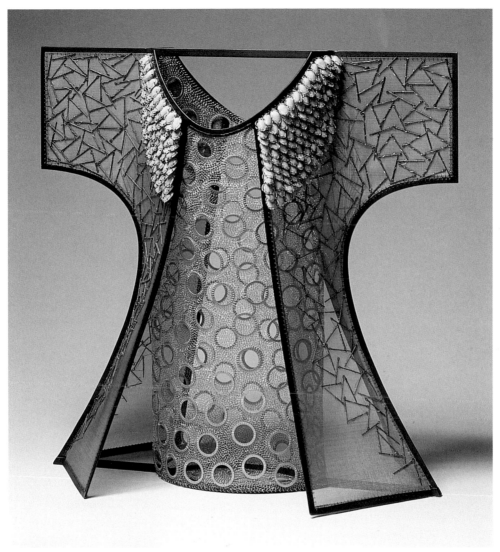

Lindsay Ketterer Rais

Kimono I | 2004

28 X 27 X 16 INCHES (71.1 X 68.6 X 40.6 CM)

Steel, stainless-steel mesh, aluminum rings, cotter pins, pistachio shells, beads; knotless netting, random stitch

PHOTOS © D. JAMES DEE

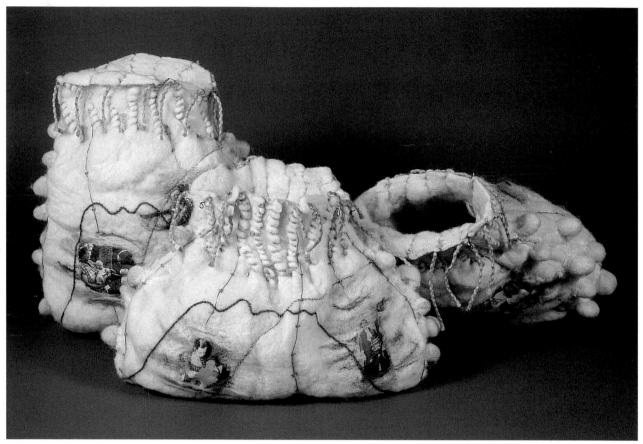

Melissa Woodburn

Female Cycles: Three Generations | 2005

12 X 21 X 14 INCHES (30.5 X 53.3 X 35.6 CM)

Wool felt, silk, cotton, wire; hand felted with shibori shaping, photo transfers, hand embroidered, couched

PHOTOS © ARTIST

Kiyomi Iwata

Torso Three | 2004

24 X 19½ X 15 INCHES (61 X 49.5 X 38.1 CM)

Dyed and stiffened silk organza, paint, wire; stitched, embellished, embroidered French knots, fabricated

PHOTO © D. JAMES DEE

Amy Mongler
Psalm 139 (3) | 2005

4½ X 7½ INCHES (11.4 X 19.1 CM)
Wool yarn, cotton thread, silk; felted knitting
PHOTO © JENNY DOWD

Manya Shapiro
Vessel | 2002

5 X 5 X 4 INCHES (12.7 X 12.7 X 10.2 CM)
Paper, pins, gold leaf; pinned, glued
PHOTO © BILL BACHHUBER

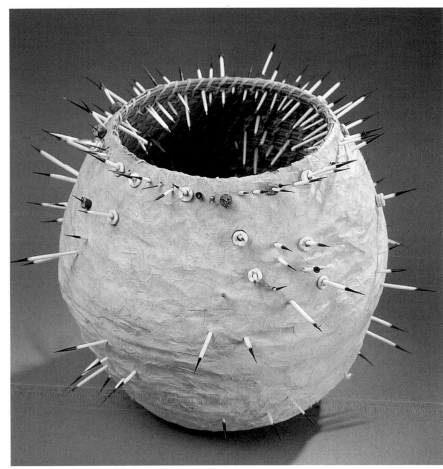

Jo-Ann Van Reeuwyk

Vortex | 2004

6 X 6 X 5 INCHES (15.2 X 15.2 X 12.7 CM)
Pine needles, raffia, handmade paper,
porcupine quills, beads; coiled, stitched

PHOTOS © JOHN CORRIVEAU

PHOTO © RUMMEL STUDIO

THE INSPIRATION *for this piece came from the beautiful weavings of the Haida Indians in the southeastern Alaska panhandle region. The design was called "Raven's Tail" by Cheryl Samuel, who re-created it from old chief's robes from the 1980s. The design under the rim was created to complement the raven's tail in the center, decorated here with beads.*

Joan Moore

Fire and Ice: Alaska Heritage | 2005

3 X 5 X 5 INCHES (7.6 X 12.7 X 12.7 CM)

Black ash, waxed linen, cotton thread; dyed, continuous-twill weaving, raven's tail weaving

Joan Moore

Indian Quilt | 1998–2005

4 X 4½ X 12 INCHES (10.2 X 11.4 X 30.5 CM)

Dyed reed; continuous-twill construction,
mountain and valley pattern

PHOTO © RUMMEL STUDIO

Elaine Robson

Covey Oval: Regal | 2004

7¼ X 12¼ X 10¼ INCHES (19.7 X 31.1 X 26 CM)

Reed, seagrass, Hamburg cane; plain and chase weave construction, four-rod coil, reverse arrow, filled cat-head bottom

PHOTO © PETER ROBSON

Peggy A. Helm

Tidal Pool | 2005

2½ X 7½ INCHES (6.4 X 19.1 CM)

Natural and dyed long-leaf pine needles, cotton thread, sea shells, glass beads, plastic rings; coiled, stitched, teneriffe weaving, wrapped

PHOTO © J. D. HAYWARD

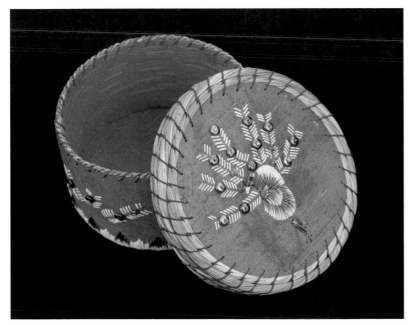

SINCE I *was a child, I have been fascinated with native Canadian quillwork on birch bark. I have used techniques from traditional quillwork, but have added iridescent glass beads to highlight the peacock's tail feathers.*

Sheila Ziman

Vanity | 2005

3 X 4½ INCHES (7.6 X 11.4 CM)

Birch bark, porcupine quills, glass beads, sweetgrass, waxed linen; quilled, stitched, coiled

PHOTO © LYN WINANS

Elizabeth J. Loftus
Undulations | 2003

4½ X 5 X 4 INCHES (11.4 X 12.7 X 10.2 CM)
Waxed linen, glass and wood beads;
twined, continuous construction
PHOTO © LANCE KEMIG

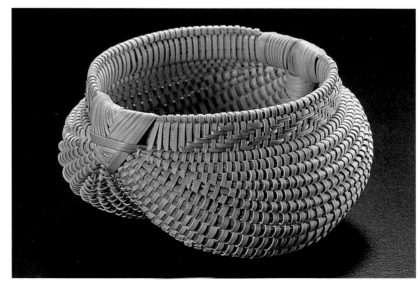

Cynthia W. Taylor
Just a Handful | 2001

2½ X 4¼ X 3½ INCHES (6.4 X 10.8 X 8.9 CM)
Hand-split white oak; rib-work construction
PHOTO © JIM OSBORN

Banbalmirr Bidingal

Bathi | 2005

27³⁄₁₆ X 21¹¹⁄₁₆ X 12⅝ INCHES (69 X 55 X 32 CM)

Pandanus palm, vegetable dye; coiled,
continuous construction

PHOTO © SASHA S. EARLE

Robin Taylor Daugherty

Square Root of X | 2004

17 X 17 X 6 INCHES (43.2 X 43.2 X 15.2 CM)

White ash, northwest sweetgrass, red- and
yellow-cedar bark, roots; plaited and twined
with imbrication and wrapping

PHOTO © KEN SANVILLE

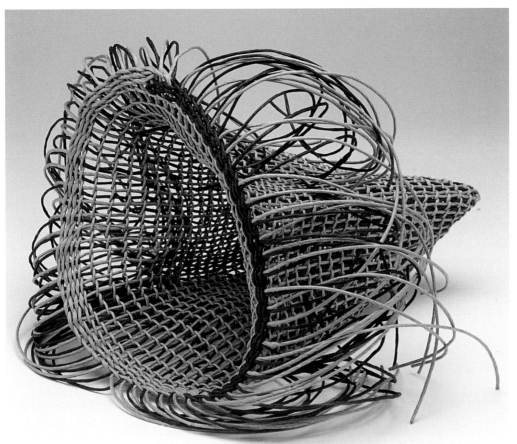

CONTRAST BETWEEN *a very regular weave and a looser form is a recurring characteristic of my work. There is an element left to chance and which is dictated by the properties of the material I have chosen to use. I am interested in the character of the line and how a subtle variation in the weave creates movement.*

Rachel Max

A Pocket Full of Air | 2004

10 X 12 X 12 INCHES (25.4 X 30.5 X 30.5 CM)
Paper string; twined

PHOTO © STEPHEN BRAYNE

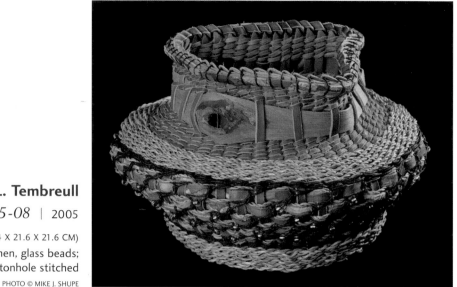

Karen L. Tembreull

Symphonic Interruption 2005-08 | 2005

5½ X 8½ X 8½ INCHES (14 X 21.6 X 21.6 CM)

Elm bark, soft-rush cordage, waxed linen, glass beads;
double bottom, twined, chased, buttonhole stitched

PHOTO © MIKE J. SHUPE

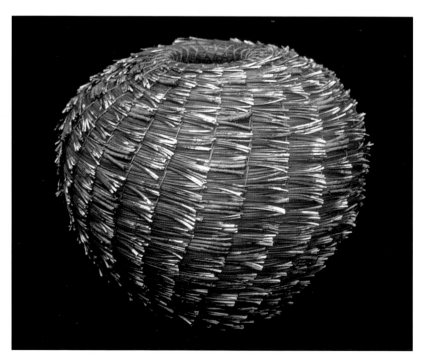

Francina Krayneh-Prince
Neil Prince

Mojave Bloom | 2003

10 X 10 X 10 INCHES (25.4 X 25.4 X 25.4 CM)

Torrey pine needles, waxed-linen cord, raffia;
dyed, coiled construction

PHOTO © ARTIST

Linda Ellis Andrews

Amethyst with Gold Lip: Optical Weave Series | 1997

6½ X 11 X 11 INCHES (16.5 X 27.9 X 27.9 CM)
Fused and kiln-formed glass rods

PHOTOS © ARTIST

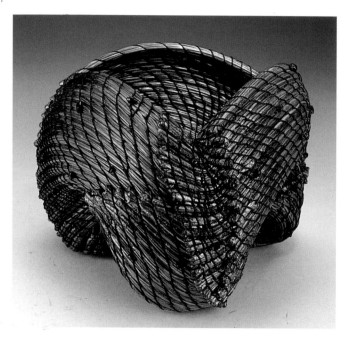

Clay Burnette

Garnet Tripod | 2004

6 X 8 X 8 INCHES (15.2 X 20.3 X 20.3 CM)

Long-leaf pine needles, waxed-linen thread, garnets, beeswax; dyed, painted, coiled construction

PHOTO © GEORGE FULTON

Beth Marek

Untitled | 2004

18 X 6 X 6 INCHES (45.7 X 15.2 X 15.2 CM)

Brass wire, glass beads; crocheted

PHOTO © LARRY SANDERS

Chris Warren

Woodland Shell | 2005

12 X 12 X 30 INCHES (30.5 X 30.5 X 76.2 CM)
Driftwood, seagrass, wild-cherry bark,
kelp; rib construction
PHOTO © BILL BACHHUBER

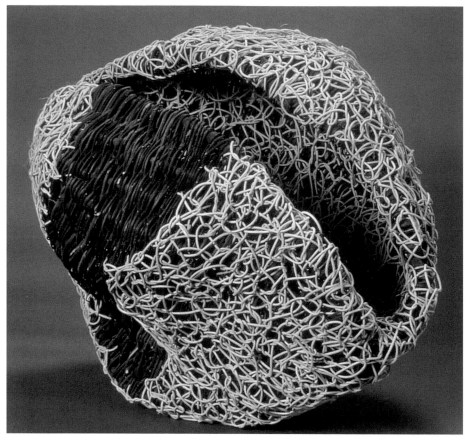

MY BASKETS *explore form, line, and texture and reflect my environment. Using primarily native Florida grapevine that I harvest at a local preserve, I construct basketry forms using both traditional and non-traditional interlacing techniques. I am a basket-maker foremost and am drawn to the purity of the vessel shape, but I am equally attentive to its potential as a sculptural object.*

Benjia Morgenstern
Untitled | 1999–2000

16 X 21 X 16 INCHES (40.6 X 53.3 X 40.6 CM)
Native Florida grapevine, reed; rib weave

PHOTOS © DON QUERALTO

Dawn Walden

Untitled | 2003

18 X 18 X 18 INCHES (45.7 X 45.7 X 45.7 CM)

Cedar bark and roots; interlaced

PHOTO © DAVID PETERS

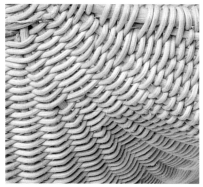

Mary Hettmansperger

Ripple Effect | 2003

18 X 22 X 34 INCHES (45.7 X 55.9 X 86.4 CM)

Round rattan, honeysuckle; rib construction

PHOTOS © JEFF BAIRD

John G. Garrett

Baroque Twist | 2004

13 X 21 X 12 INCHES
(33 X 53.3 X 30.5 CM)

Copper, hardware cloth;
personal technique

PHOTO © MARGO GEIST

Lauren Bristol

Brigid's Circle | 2004

11 X 20 X 19 INCHES (27.9 X 50.8 X 48.3 CM)

Egyptian cotton, cotton, wood, beads,
fiber core; coiled, carved, sanded,
twisted, bead stringing

PHOTO © JOHN DOWLING

221

THIS WORK *was constructed using a Norfolk Island plait, traditionally used for making hats. By virtue of their shape, these baskets are rendered useless, hence the title in the Norfolk language of this South Pacific island where I live.*

Margarita Sampson
Strange Fruit: Handy Es a Closet Gut No Moel | 2004

22 X 7⅞ X 7⅞ INCHES (56 X 20 X 20 CM)
Corn husks, guava stick, four-plait construction

PHOTO © ARTIST

I DELIGHT *in turning throwaway mail, such as catalogs, into organic forms.*

Ellen Jantzen

TriVessel Form | 2003

12 X 12 INCHES (30.5 X 30.5 CM)
Recycled mail-order catalogs,
silver sage twigs; papier-mâché

PHOTO © ARTIST

Robyn Djunginy

Pandanus Bottles | 2004

LEFT: 18⅛ X 4⅓ INCHES (46 X 11 CM);
CENTER: 15⅜ X 11⁷⁄₁₆ INCHES (39 X 29 CM);
RIGHT: 19⁵⁄₁₆ X 8¼ INCHES (49 X 21 CM)

Pandanus spiralis (screw palm), vegetable-root
dyes; coil-weave technique

PHOTO © BELINDA SCOTT

INSPIRATION FOR *this vessel is from natural forms, particularly tree roots as they twine about on the ground and around stones.*

Ed Bing Lee

Roots | 2004

6 X 6 X 6 INCHES (15.2 X 15.2 X 15.2 CM)
Cotton, raffia, linen, waxed linen
PHOTO © KEN YANNOAK

Michal A. Costello

Twisty Ways of Wisdom | 2004

11 X 8¼ X 8½ INCHES (27.9 X 21 X 21.6 CM)
Pine needles, glass beads, waxed linen; coiled
PHOTO © LARRY NUZUM

Ane Lyngsgaard

Untitled | 2005

39¾ X 47¼ X 59¹⁄₁₆ INCHES (100 X 120 X 150 CM)

Willow, bark; single-woven construction,
based on a Catalan base

PHOTO © RASMUS STENGAARD

Polly Adams Sutton

Onyx | 2004

7 X 11 X 37 INCHES (17.8 X 27.9 X 94 CM)

Cedar bark, ash, wire, cane; woven, twined

PHOTO © WENDY MCEAHERN

Marlene Burrunali

Untitled | 2003

8²⁄₃ X 17¹⁄₃ X 15 INCHES (22 X 44 X 38 CM)
Hand-dyed pandanus; coiled

PHOTOS © RODNEY START

Wendy Namarnyilk

Bucket | 2002

8¼ X 15⅜ X 11 INCHES (21 X 39 X 28 CM)
Hand-dyed pandanus; coiled, plaited

PHOTO © RODNEY START

Marilyn Gumurdul

Badjkid | 2004

10¼ X 18⅞ X 13 INCHES (26 X 48 X 33 CM)
Hand-dyed pandanus; coiled

PHOTO © RODNEY START

Sylvia White

Blue Envelope | 2005

36 X 11 X 6½ INCHES (91.4 X 27.9 X 16.5 CM)

Computer wire, strapping tape, plastic grid; shaped, woven

PHOTOS © FRANK ROSS

I AM *fascinated by the way fabric drapes against the female form, and I was inspired by the way artists have depicted this, whether on ancient stone statues, or in clothing and costumes. I wanted to see the effect I could create by embellishing a knotted form with a beaded sheath, contrasting and complementing the sleekness of the "skin" with the folds of the "fabric."*

Merrill Morrison

Goddess | 2004

8½ X 3 INCHES (21.6 X 7.6 CM)
Waxed linen, glass beads; knotted,
right-angle bead weaving

PHOTOS © DAVID PETERS

Elizabeth Whyte Schulze

Bitter Lemon | 2004

14 X 19½ X 14 INCHES (35.6 X 49.5 X 35.6 CM)
Pine needles, raffia, acrylic paint; coiled
PHOTO © JOHN POLAK

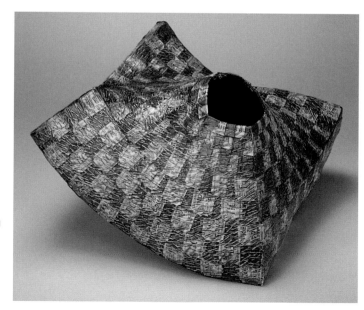

Stephen Johnson

Flame Boy | 2005

10 X 13 X 13 INCHES (25.4 X 33 X 33 CM)
Paper, shoe polish, staples
PHOTO © DAMIAN JOHNSON

Susan Taber Avila

B. Cielo | 2004

21½ X 18 X 10½ INCHES (54.6 X 45.7 X 26.7 CM)

Thread, digitally-printed silk charmeuse, industrial felt, sequins; hand and machine stitched

PHOTOS © LEE FATHERREE

Judith Boesky

Spheres of Influence | 2002

OVERALL: 1¼ X 5 FEET (0.4 X 1.5 M)

Bamboo, reed, cane, handmade paper, seagrass, hemp, fiber rush; random weave

PHOTOS © TIM THAYER

Aaron Kramer

Egg | 2005

30 X 20 X 20 INCHES (76.2 X 50.8 X 50.8 CM)

Recycled hardwoods, street-sweeper bristles, car parts, welded armature; random weave

PHOTOS © ARTIST

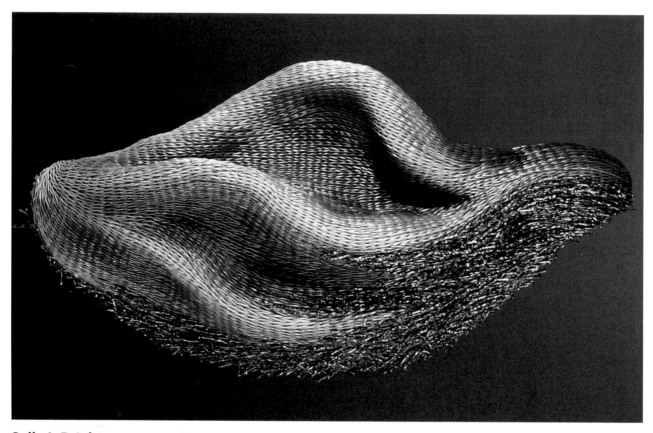

Sally J. Bright

Time Expanded | 2004

48 X 30 X 15 INCHES (121.9 X 76.2 X 38.1 CM)

Rattan, palm, wood backing, paint;
hand woven, painted

PHOTO © ARTIST

Danielle Bodine

Migration–Transport Series | 2004

8 X 3 X 3 INCHES (20.3 X 7.6 X 7.6 CM)

Mulberry paper, wire, plastic, toothpicks, hair, metal; cast, coiled, manipulated, painted, stamped, collaged, embellished, burned

PHOTO © MICHAEL STADLER

MY FLAX-AND-PAPER *vessel basket forms are an homage to fiber artist Kay Sekimachi.*

Andrea Tucker-Hody

Camel-Hair Tale | 2004

9 X 3¼ X 2½ INCHES (22.9 X 8.3 X 6.4 CM)

Flax and kozo fiber, hand-dyed camel hair, brass base; drape molded

PHOTO © GEORGE POST

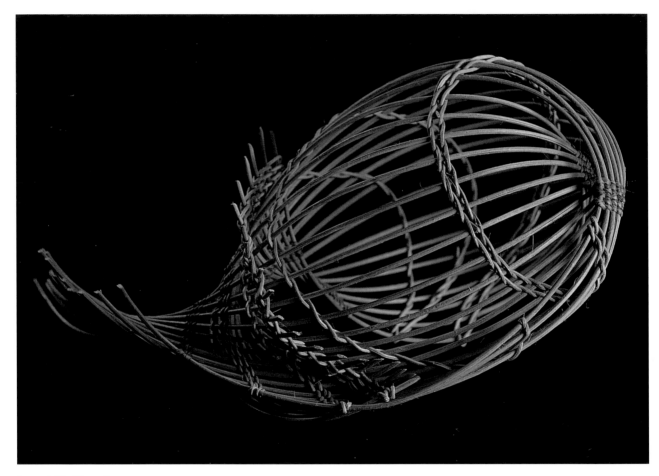

Janet B. Reed

Spiral Series: Conch VIII | 2004

6 X 5 X 11 INCHES (15.2 X 12.7 X 33 CM)

Reed/rattan, raffia, onion skins; dyed, twined

PHOTO © JON MEAD

A MOON moth from Madagascar was the inspiration for this piece—one in a series based on cocoon shapes. The medium I choose to work in is horsehair, which I enjoy for its translucency, design opportunities, and ability to create a firm architectural shape with a single fine material.

Amanda Salm

Luna | 2003

6½ X 12 X 5 INCHES (16.5 X 30.5 X 12.7 CM)
Horsehair, natural dyes; coiled
PHOTOS © DORIAN JON

239

Mary Giles

Evening Reflections | 2004

13¾ X 30 X 7 INCHES (34.9 X 76.2 X 17.8 CM)

Waxed linen, iron, copper; coiled

PHOTOS © TONY DECK

Karyl Sisson

Tropism | 2003

4 X 5 INCHES (10.2 X 12.7 CM)
Vintage metal hairpins, safety
pins, wire; twined
PHOTO © SUSAN EINSTEIN

Merrill Morrison

Iced Tea | 2003

6¾ X 9¾ X 6 INCHES (17.1 X 24.8 X 15.2 CM)
Waxed linen, glass beads; knotted
PHOTO © BERNARD WOLF

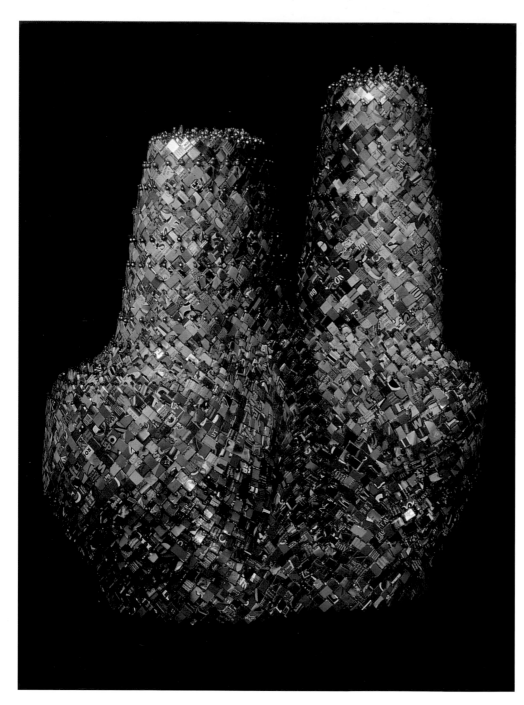

Amy Lipshie

S/He | 2004

30 X 24 X 17 INCHES
(76.2 X 61 X 43.2 CM)

Cereal boxes, beads, glue,
nylon thread, polymer
varnish; cut, folded,
chained, glued, sewn

PHOTOS © DIANA LYN

David Paul Bacharach

Silo | 2003

48 X 15 X 15 INCHES (121.9 X 38.1 X 38.1 CM)
Copper sheet; cut, plaited, patinated
PHOTO © NORMAN WATKINS

Jeffrey Lloyd Dever

Progeny | 2004

18 X 4½ X 4½ INCHES (45.7 X 11.4 X 11.4 CM)

Plastic-coated copper wire, polymer; fabricated, wrapped, woven, drilled, carved, back filled

PHOTOS © GREGORY R. STALEY

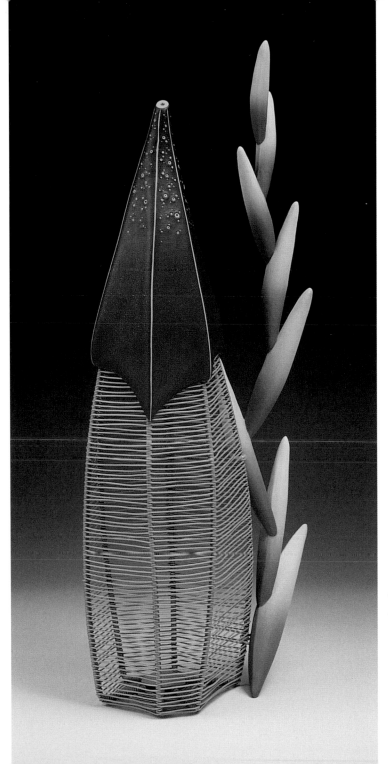

THE GOAL *of all my work, whether jewelry, vessels, or baskets, is to explore sculptural form and to investigate the intersection of contrast and harmony—in color, texture, and structure. I also enjoy the challenge of taking simple, inexpensive, easily accessible materials and creating objects of desire, valued for their innovative and aesthetic qualities rather than their material worth.*

Jeffrey Lloyd Dever
Autumnal Repose | 2005

18 X 6 X 4 INCHES (45.7 X 15.2 X 10.2 CM)
Steel wire, plastic-coated copper wire, polymer; fabricated polymer shell over continuous wire-wrapped woven basket, attached reinforced polymer branch, drilled, carved, back filled
PHOTO © GREGORY R. STALEY

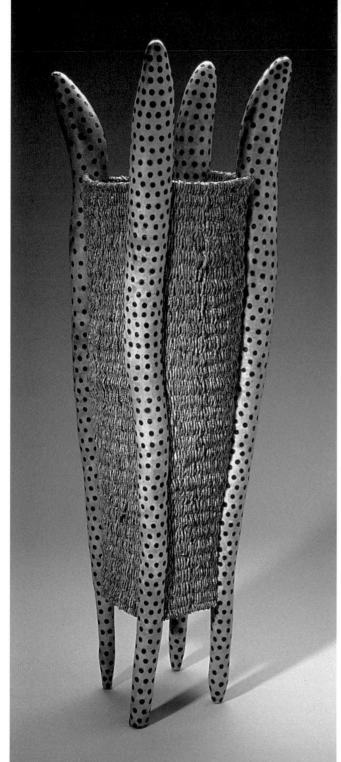

Don Weeke

Dot Column | 2002

47¼ X 16½ X 16½ INCHES (120 X 41.9 X 41.9 CM)

Gourd, reed, palm frond; woven, pyrography

PHOTOS © RODNEY NAKAMOTO

Polly Adams Sutton

Pearl | 2004

12 X 10 X 29 INCHES (30.5 X 25.4 X 73.7 CM)
Cedar bark, beads, wire; woven
PHOTO © BILL WICKETT

Shelly DeChantal

Pleated Vessel: Open | 2004

7 X 8 X 30 INCHES (17.8 X 20.3 X 76.2 CM)
Silk, aluminum mesh, cotton, stone, wire, glass
beads, metallic thread; hand painted, shibori
dyed, hand formed, fabric manipulation, beaded
PHOTO © JOHN BONATH

247

I MADE *each piece separately, and when I put them together they seemed to hug each other, creating a nice negative space as well.*

Dona Anderson

The Embrace | 2005

22 X 13 X 8 INCHES (55.9 X 33 X 20.3 CM)
Round reed, paint, Japanese print paper; sewn
PHOTO © BILL WICKETT

Dorothy Gill Barnes

Spiral | 1987

16 X 7 INCHES DIAMETER (40.6 X 17.8 CM)

Poplar, pine

PHOTO © DOUG MARTIN
COURTESY DEL MANO GALLERY

Jill Nordfors Clark

Totem Rising | 2004

42½ X 11½ INCHES (108 X 29.2 CM)

Hog gut, vine rattan, parachute cord;
double layered, dyed, stitched, coiled

Sally Shore

Opera Bag | 2004

7¼ X 7 X 4¾ INCHES (18.4 X 17.8 X 12.1 CM)

Ribbon, glass beads, satin lining; tri-axial weaving, beaded with fringe, machine and hand sewn

PHOTO © ARTIST

Jan Zicarelli

Orange Blossom Beaded Basket | 2002

2½ X 3 X 3 INCHES (6.4 X 7.6 X 7.6 CM)

Seed beads, nylon thread; bead-weaving techniques

PHOTO © ROBIN STANCLIFF

MY VESSELS *refer to the female form as the bearer of human experiences and the conveyer of culture through time. I choose silk cloth to work with because of its sensuous, supple qualities.*

Shelly DeChantal
Pleated Vessel: One | 2004

14½ X 7 X 19½ INCHES (36.8 X 17.8 X 49.5 CM)

Silk, aluminum mesh, cotton, stone, glass beads; hand painted, shibori dyed, hand formed, fabric manipulation, beaded

PHOTOS © JOHN BONATH

Lone Villaume

Organized Disorder | 2004

7¹⁄₁₆ X 19¹¹⁄₁₆ X 6⁵⁄₁₆ INCHES (18 X 50 X 16 CM)

Rubber from bicycle tubes, iron skeleton; woven

PHOTO © OLE AKHOS

Jennifer Rife

No. 702 Vessel | 2005

14¾ X 14½ X 14½ INCHES (37.5 X 36.8 X 36.8 CM)

Silk noil, paper core, leather, leather lacing; hand dyed, torn, coiled, painted

PHOTOS © ARTIST

Pamela E. Becker
Untitled | 2005

13 X 10⅝ X 10⅝ INCHES (33 X 27 X 27 CM)
Linen and rayon thread, reed;
wrapped-coil construction
PHOTO © ARTIST

Yukari Kikuchi
Curl Up 05-1 | 2005

9 X 9 X 5⅞ INCHES (23 X 23 X 15 CM)
Phellodendron amurense (cork tree); plaited
PHOTO © ARTIST

THIS PIECE *was a happy revolution for me with the use of multiple starts in the base and the body. Since working on this, I have sketched out pages and pages of ideas for future forms.*

Amanda Salm
Swirl | 2004

7 X 6 X 3 INCHES (17.8 X 15.2 X 7.6 CM)
Horsehair, natural dyes; coiled

PHOTOS © DORIAN JON

THE INTERACTION
between the shrink-ing qualities of the handmade onion-skin paper with the ribs of chair cane creates a dynamic tension.

Shuna Rendel

On Edge | 2003

17⁵⁄₁₆ X 16⁹⁄₁₆ X 14³⁄₁₆ INCHES
(44 X 42 X 36 CM)

Dyed chair cane, onionskins, flax, handmade paper; manipulated

PHOTO © TAMSIN RENDEL

257

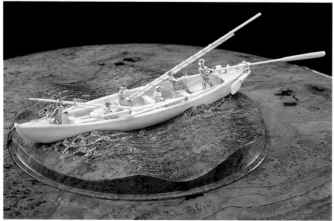

Fred C. Ely

Nantucket Sleigh Ride | 2004

7 X 16 INCHES DIAMETER (17.8 X 40.6 CM)

Cherry, cherry burl, cane, porcupine quills, ivory, 14k gold; woven, dyed, overlaid, carved, cast

PHOTOS © DON RUTT

THIS BASKET *is an abstract representation of human form and emotion. The shape, developed stick by stick, mimics nature's growth process.*

Christine Joy
Steadfast | 2005

36 X 24 X 18 INCHES (91.4 X 61 X 45.7 CM)
Willow; interlacing construction
PHOTO © DEAN ADAMS

Michael Davis

Medieval Pinecone 2004 | 2004

14 X 18 X 18 INCHES (35.6 X 45.7 X 45.7 CM)

Reed, enamel, acrylic paint, pine cone,
petals, wood; twined

PHOTO © DELOYE BURRELL

Biba Schutz

Sea Forms | 1993

5 X 14 X 6 INCHES (12.7 X 35.6 X 15.2 CM)

Patinated copper wire; constructed, wrapped

PHOTO © RON BOSZKO

THE INSPIRATION *for this basket came from Mt. Waialeale in Hawaii, the wettest spot on earth. Inside its crater, hundreds of waterfalls glisten like women's hair. The date-palm stalks represent the clouds that clothe the mountain crater.*

Mizu

Wahine O'Waialeale | 2004

15½ X 15 X 14 INCHES (39.4 X 38.1 X 35.6 CM)
Pine needles, date-palm seed stalks, carved gourd; coiled
PHOTO © RONALD KOSEN

Ruth Greenberg

Keyhole | 1998

1½ X 2¼ X 1½ INCHES (3.8 X 5.8 X 3.8 CM)

Bindweed, driftwood

PHOTO © DAVID PETERS
COURTESY DEL MANO GALLERY

Anna S. King

Smoking | 2005

2⁵⁄₁₆ X 5½ INCHES (5.5 X 14 CM)

Pine needles, waxed cotton, stone; coiled

PHOTO © SHANNON TOFTS

Mark Caluneo

Arizona | 2003

30 X 6 X 7 INCHES (76.2 X 15.2 X 17.8 CM)
Steel-diamond lathe, copper-stranded wire, brass
turnings, patina; crushing technique, wrapped, woven

PHOTOS © PETER SAN CHIRICO

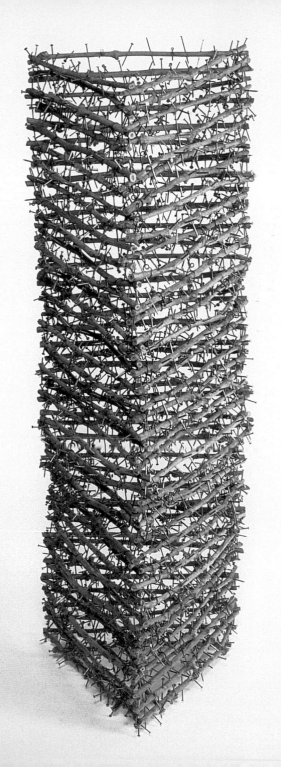

Gyöngy Laky

Trinity | 2004

40 X 13½ X 12 INCHES (101.6 X 34.3 X 30.5 CM)
Grape vine, vinyl-coated nails, steel wire; tied
PHOTO © BENJAMIN BLACKWELL

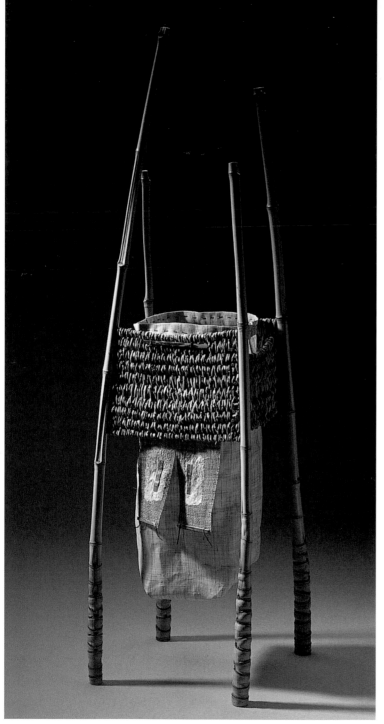

THIS WORK *was inspired by the Japanese* noren, *a gentle fabric hanging in a doorway or entry.*

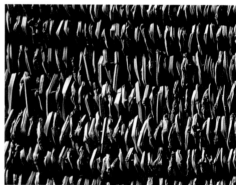

Polly Jacobs Giacchina
Noren | 2005

37 X 10 X 10 INCHES (94 X 25.4 X 25.4 CM)
Date palm, bamboo, natural fabrics, paper; sewn, twined
PHOTOS © RODNEY NAKAMOTO

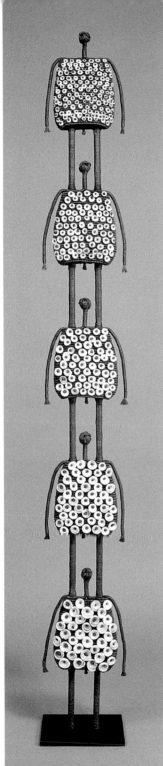

Mary Giles

Beach Totem | 2001

64 X 7 X 2½ INCHES (162.6 X 17.8 X 6.4 CM)

Waxed linen, shells, gesso, wax; coiled

PHOTOS © TONY DECK

Mary Giles

River Bark Artifact | 2003

36 X 9 X 3 INCHES (91.4 X 22.9 X 7.6 CM)

Waxed linen, tin, copper, lead; coiled

PHOTO © TONY DECK

Susan kavicky

Solar Wind | 2005

15 X 21 X 16 INCHES (38.1 X 53.3 X 40.6 CM)

Brown ash, illustration board, acrylic paint, rattan;
plaited, twilled, double-wall construction

PHOTOS © LARRY SANDERS

REVEALED BY *the arduous pounding of the tree and tedious splitting of the splints is a lush, satiny surface. Though I no longer process the material myself, I am no less inspired. As I maintain a student relationship to the work, a true communion occurs, and it is through that communion that the tree is transformed, as am I.*

Susan kavicky

Esoteric Connectedness | 2001

9½ X 42 X 16½ INCHES (24.1 X 106.7 X 41.9 CM)
Brown ash, elm bark, maple, serviceberry;
plaited, twilled, pegged, lashed

PHOTOS © LARRY SANDERS

Marc Jenesel
Karen E. Pierce

Sea, Sand & Sun | 2004

17 X 24 INCHES (43.2 X 61 CM)

Raku-fired pottery, rattan, marbled paper,
copper wire, metal leaf, palm inflorescence,
waxed linen, shells; hand dyed, four-rod
wale, stitched, thrown, altered

PHOTO © MARC JENESEL

Gerri Johnson-McMillin

Caribbean | 2004

8 X 8 X 8 INCHES (20.3 X 20.3 X 20.3 CM)
Albacore fishbone, monofilament, glass
beads; double-basket woven

PHOTO © ARTIST

IN MY constructions, *individually beautiful, but fragile, feathers are assembled into strong vessels. Like elegant chariots, soft yet secure, they are destined to carry a soul on its transmigration into the next world.*

C. A. Michel
Soliloquy | 2004

10½ X 3 INCHES (26.7 X 7.6 CM)
Peacock and pheasant feathers, wool, linen core; coiled
PHOTO © ROGER SCHREIBER

C. A. Michel
Untitled | 2003

8 X 3 INCHES (20.3 X 7.6 CM)
Pheasant feathers, wool, linen core; coiled
PHOTO © ROGER SCHREIBER

Flo Hoppe

Shahzada | 2004

8 X 16½ INCHES (20.3 X 41.9 CM)

Dyed rattan, Japanese and Malaysian cane;
double-basket technique, twined,
embroidered, embellished

ALL OF *my work honors and celebrates the family. Nana Doll is my favorite piece. I sit in a birthing chair, cradling my two grandsons, Blake and Cody, in a basket while baby Heather swings below.*

Judy Mulford
Nana Doll | 1998

11 ¼ X 8 X 4 INCHES (30 X 20.3 X 10.2 CM)

Waxed linen, polymer clay, antique buttons, pounded tin-can lids, beads, plastic, fine silver; looped

PHOTOS © SUSAN EINSTEIN

WHILE I *am simplifying my life, my pieces are becoming more complex. The seventeen figures here are built on knives, forks, and spoons made from tin to sterling silver, depicting all economic levels. They are an ever-changing flower arrangement as they push to an unknown future.*

Judy Mulford

We're All in This Boat Together | 2003

12 X 21 X 12 INCHES (30.5 X 53.3 X 30.5 CM)

Gourd, waxed linen, fine silver, pearls, beads, knives, forks, spoons, polymer clay, pounded tin-can lids, antique buttons; knotted, looped

PHOTOS © BILL DEWEY

Lizzie Farey

Eulogy | 2003

13⅜ X 11 X 11 INCHES (34 X 28 X 28 CM)
Steamed willow, preserved catkins; contemporary
random-weave construction

PHOTO © SHANNON TOFTS

Rob Dobson

Basket #106 | 2002

15 X 15 X 10 INCHES (38.1 X 38.1 X 25.4 CM)

Perforated aluminum scrap, galvanized duct cap, wood,
bx cable, pipe brackets, black and chrome-plated plastic,
beads, screws, nuts, washers; constructed

PHOTO © JEFF BAIRD

CURRENTLY I *am using silicon bronze as my primary medium. The ductility of soft annealed bronze makes it similar to the pliable plant fibers that are commonly used in basketry. Additionally, the property of rapid-work hardening makes the finished form hard and strong, equivalent to the hardening that occurs when plant fibers are dried.*

Ema Tanigaki

Vaseform Basket | 2005

10½ X 8½ X 8½ INCHES (26.7 X 21.6 X 21.6 CM)

Silicon bronze, bronze wire; hand wrought, welded, drilled, attached, hand formed, tendril weave technique, patinated, lacquered, waxed

PHOTO © JOHN L. HEALEY

Jerry Bleem

Float | 2004

12 X 16 X 11½ INCHES (30.5 X 40.6 X 29.2 CM)

Fish scales, staples; accretion by stapling

PHOTO © TOM VAN EYNDE

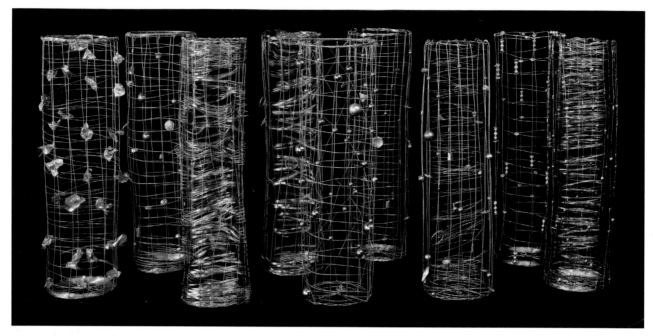

Sally Prangley

Strength | 2005

EACH: 4 X 16 INCHES (10.2 X 40.6 CM)

Stainless-steel wires, found metal objects and beads; wire worked, continuous-construction technique

PHOTO © ART GRICE

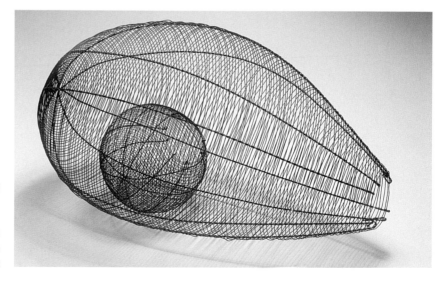

Briana-Lyn Syvarth

#1 | 2001

20 X 19 X 26 INCHES (50.8 X 48.3 X 66 CM)

Steel wire; tinkering technique

PHOTO © D. JAMES DEE

THE FIGURE *in the center foreground has been bronzed; the others are willow and I may cast them in bronze in the future. There's always the chance that original works in willow may be burned out or "lost" in the conversion to bronze.*

Dawn MacNutt

Return to Delos | 1999–2004

5 TO 7 FEET (1.8 TO 2.1 M) HIGH
Willow, seagrass; twined, bronzed
PHOTO © ARTIST

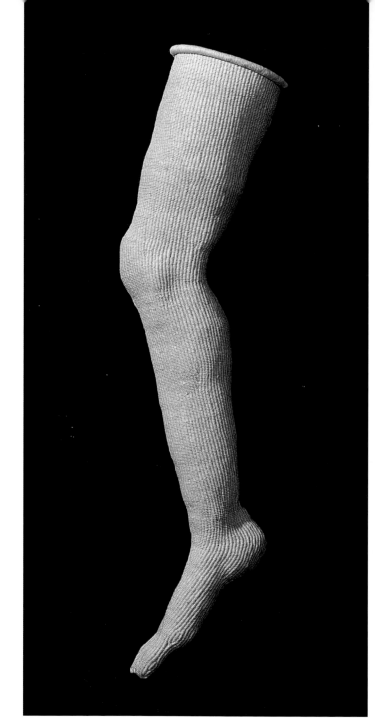

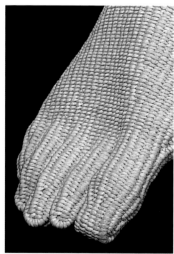

Ann Coddington Rast

milagro: leg | 2005

36 X 8 X 6 INCHES (91.4 X 20.3 X 15.2 CM)

Linen; twined

PHOTOS © WILMER ZEHR

IN THIS *work I attempted to capture a momentary gesture of tenderness, a connection between parts of the self, or between two people— a gesture of unity.*

Ann Coddington Rast

join hands | 2004

30 X 14 X 12 INCHES (76.2 X 35.6 X 30.5 CM)
Linen; twined

PHOTOS © WILMER ZEHR

F. Carol Stein

Patient Stone | 2005

13 X 9 X 4½ INCHES (33 X 22.9 X 11.4 CM)

Rice paper, pastels, seagrass, waxed linen, beads; coiled, sewn

PHOTO © ANDY EDGAR

F. Carol Stein

Endora # II | 2004

22 X 20 X 9 INCHES (55.9 X 50.8 X 22.9 CM)

Rice paper, pastels, seagrass,
waxed linen; sewn, coiled

PHOTO © ANDREW EDGAR

WIRE HAS *a mind of its own sometimes. I've learned to let it take me to its own end.*

Laura Balombini

Winter's End Dance | 2004

28 X 12 X 12 INCHES (71.1 X 30.5 X 30.5 CM)
Steel wire, polymer clay; hand woven, sculpted
PHOTO © JEFF BAIRD

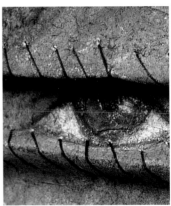

Carol Stein

Watchful Waiting #4 | 2004

45 X 30 X 17 INCHES (114.3 X 76.2 X 43.2 CM)

Rice paper, waxed linen, pastels,
seagrass, beads; sewn, coiled

PHOTOS © ARTIST

Barbara J. Walker

Ronnzini's Magical Mystery Tour | 2004

6 X 8 X 3¾ INCHES (15.2 X 20.3 X 9.5 CM)

Four-ply cotton and metallic cords, needle-felted wool balls, silk scarves, hardwood wand (all materials made by artist); ply-split, doubled Chinese button knots, wrapped

PHOTO © BRIAN MCLERNON

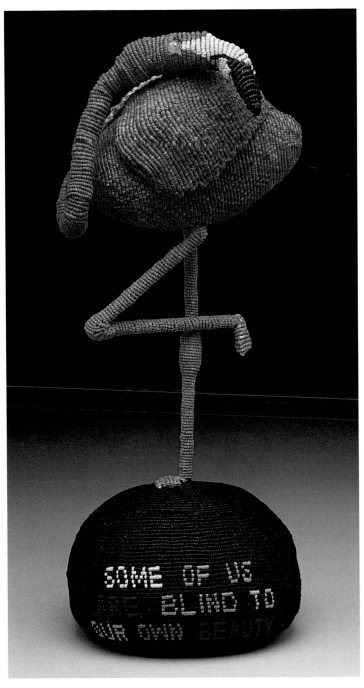

THE TEXT *on this piece is: "Some of us are blind to our own beauty; some of us are blind to our own faults."*

Leah Danberg

Balancing Act | 2004

14 X 5½ X 5 INCHES (35.6 X 14 X 12.7 CM)

Waxed linen, cotton, polystyrene foam; knotted

PHOTO © GEORGE POST

Leah Danberg

Sing Out | 2003

14 X 12½ X 4½ INCHES (35.6 X 31.8 X 11.4 CM)

Waxed linen, cotton, polystyrene foam; knotted

PHOTOS © BERNARD WOLF

Lois Russell

Fiddlesticks # 1 | 2002

11 X 3 X 3 INCHES (27.9 X 7.6 X 7.6 CM)
Waxed linen; twined, wrapped, stitched

PHOTO © JEFF MAGIDSON

Mary Hettmansperger

Waste Not, Want Not | 2003

19 X 8 X 8 INCHES (48.3 X 20.3 X 20.3 CM)
Waxed linen, found objects; full-twist twined

PHOTO © JEFF BAIRD

THESE THREE *individually woven cylindrical shapes that are attached together represent the strength and unity of family.*

Phyllis Walla Catania
Triple Totem | 2004

36 X 8½ INCHES (91.4 X 21.6 CM)
Datu rattan, waxed linen; hand split, continuously woven, knotted, twined
PHOTO © JERRY ANTHONY

Leandra Spangler

Reclamation | 2004

23½ X 6½ X 6½ INCHES (59.7 X 16.5 X 16.5 CM)

Reed, handmade paper, birch bark, antique barbed wire, glass beads

PHOTOS © HELIOS STUDIO

Sally Metcalf

Untitled | 2005

13 X 11 X 12 INCHES (33 X 27.9 X 30.5 CM)
Maple bark, branches, seagrass, iris,
copper wire, washers; folded, pinned,
twined, patinated
PHOTO © ARTIST

Virginia Kaiser

Safe Within | 2002

HEIGHT: 15⅜ INCHES (39 CM)
Jacaranda, date palm fruit stalks; stitched with linen
PHOTO © GREG PIPER

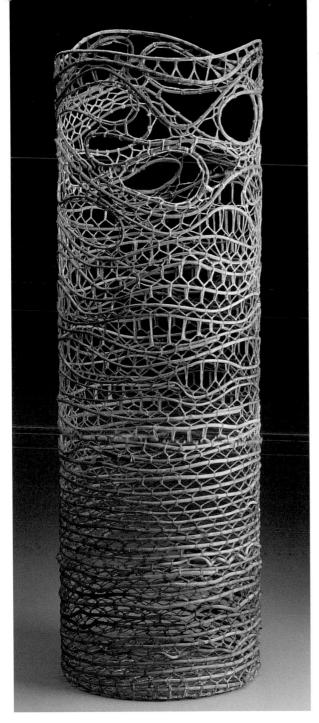

SOAKED VINE *rattan and wet hog casings are as pliable as cooked fettuccini. Together these materials can create a drawing tool as versatile as any pencil.*

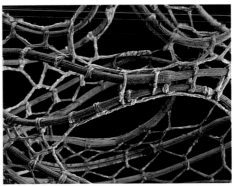

Jill Nordfors Clark
Line Drawing II | 2003

30 X 9½ INCHES (76.2 X 22.9 CM)
Hog gut, vine rattan; stitched, coiled

PHOTOS © TOM HOLT

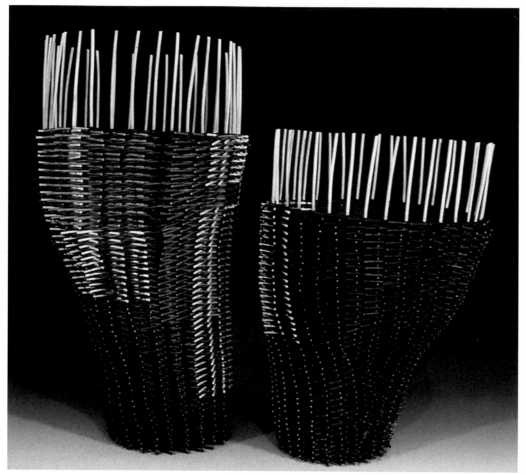

THIS IS *the first non-symmetrical basket I've woven with the human body as its reference. "He" stands there rigid, in full control of himself. "She" stands there, equally strong but full of curves and emotions (reds), popping out here and there. Placed facing each other, she meets an immovable wall and the situation is static, but turn her, and all sorts of wonderful stories are possible.*

Kari Lonning
She Met a Wall, and Other Stories | 2004

LEFT (HE): 18½ X 9 X 11 INCHES (47 X 22.9 X 27.9 CM);
RIGHT (SHE): 14½ X 9½ X 10 INCHES (36.8 X 24.1 X 25.4 CM)
Dyed rattan reed; four-rod wale and "hairy" technique

PHOTO © ARTIST

IN THIS *basket, the idea of nature—diagonals, gardens, feminine— meets technology—rigid verticals, computers, and the masculine.*

Kari Lonning

Nature Meets Technology | 2005

20¾ X 14½ X 14½ INCHES (52.7 X 36.8 X 36.8 CM)

Artist-dyed rattan reed; live-rod wale and "hairy" technique

PHOTO © ARTIST

Jenny Dowd

Roly-Poly Basketcases | 2001

SMALLEST: 8 X 7½ X 4½ INCHES
(20.3 X 19.1 X 11.4 CM);
LARGEST: 9 X 6 X 4½ INCHES
(22.9 X 15.2 X 11.4 CM)

Stoneware, paper clay, terra sigillata
slip; hand built, pit fired

PHOTO © ARTIST

Shuji Ikeda

Woodfired Tsuchi-Kago | 2004

11 X 11 X 11 INCHES (27.9 X 27.9 X 27.9 CM)
Slab and hand-built clay; braided, wood fired

PHOTO © BLACK CAT STUDIO

THIS WORK *was inspired by two very large seagulls that distracted me as I stood at my kitchen window one morning. The shadow they created as they circled, hovering over our back yard, pestered and pestered me until I finally looked up and took notice of them. They moved one above the other in a playful fashion, courting and enjoying the warmth of the sun. When I went out to the studio to work on the piece I had started the night before, I suddenly saw in it the two birds, one above the other, her soaring above, him pursuing but at the same time supporting.*

Sharon Breckenridge

She Flies Above | 2001

10½ X 20 X 11 INCHES (26.7 X 50.8 X 27.9 CM)
Seagrass, reed; space dyed, rib construction
on cedar-root handle

PHOTO © JOHN NISTICO

John G. Garrett

Harmonies | 2004

10 X 43 X 10 INCHES
(25.4 X 109.2 X 25.4 CM)

Copper, hardware cloth, copper tubing, piano strings, plied fabric, wire; personal techniques

PHOTO © MARGO GEIST

Lei McCornack

Waves | 2004

8½ X 14 INCHES (21.6 X 35.6 CM)

Seagrass, seashells; twined, tri-lobed

PHOTO © DAVID STONE

Will Pergl

Shell | 1997

52 X 47 X 30 INCHES (132.1 X 119.4 X 76.2 CM)

Oak, copper; bent-wood lamination

PHOTOS © ARTIST

Phyllis Walla Catania

Open Box | 2004

11 X 14½ X 3 INCHES (27.9 X 36.8 X 7.6 CM)
Datu rattan, waxed linen; hand split,
woven, knotted, twined

PHOTO © JERRY ANTHONY

Betty Edwards
Untitled | 2005

EACH: 5½ X 3¾ X 5 INCHES
(14 X 9.5 X 12.7 CM)
Seed beads, wire; loom woven
PHOTO © SALLY O'RILEY

Betty Edwards
Untitled | 2005

6 X 5 X 7 INCHES (15.2 X 12.7 X 17.8 CM)
Seed beads, wire; loom woven
PHOTO © SALLY O'RILEY

THIS BASKET *is based on the Greek goddess Arachne myth. The bottom of the basket is open to enter the spider's "nest." As I am also a storyteller, I base much of my work on folklore.*

Rosemarie Hohol

Arachne: The Nest | 2001

19 X 10 X 10 INCHES (48.3 X 25.4 X 25.4 CM)
Reed, wire; hand dyed, double-wall
continuous construction

PHOTO © ROGER HAUGE

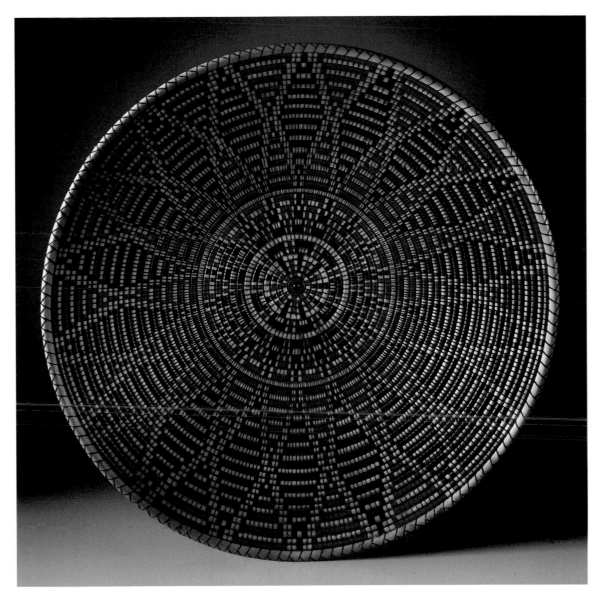

David Nittmann

Cabalitos de Flor (The Flower Merry-Go-Round) | 2004

20 X 3 INCHES (50.8 X 7.6 CM)

European pear; bowl formed, turned, burned, dyed

PHOTO © BENKO PHOTOGRAPHICS

A **BASKET** *doesn't always have to enclose a void. This willow skeleton surrounds a mass of loose sisal, and the opening is plugged with a circle of handmade paper.*

Michele Hament
Untitled | 2000

14 X 12 X 2½ INCHES (35.6 X 30.5 X 6.4 CM)
Willow, dyed reed, sisal, handmade
paper, waxed linen, gold thread;
lashed, woven, wrapped

PHOTO © ARTIST

Victoria James

Tall Lidded Jar | 2004

8¼ X 5½ INCHES (21 X 14 CM)
Pine needles, waxed linen,
polymer clay; coiled, hand built
PHOTO © RICHARD REID

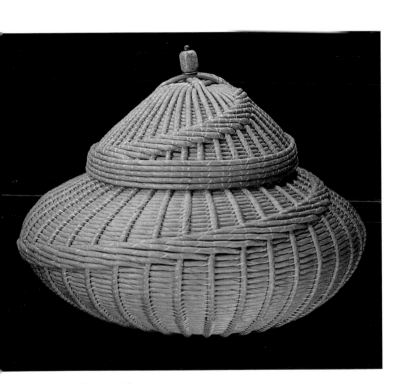

Marilyn J. Sharp

Natural Swirl | 2004

10 X 13 INCHES (25.4 X 33 CM)
Fiber rush, waxed thread, stone bead; wrapped twining
PHOTO © RUDOLF SHARP

Ruth Boland

Squares and Rectangles | 2003

16 X 12 X 12 INCHES (40.6 X 30.5 X 30.5 CM)
Reed, waxed linen; hand-dyed twill
PHOTO © ARTIST

Mary M. Miller

Space | 2005

15 X 9 X 9 INCHES (38.1 X 22.9 X 22.9 CM)
Paper, paint, waxed linen; plaited
PHOTO © STEPHEN PETEGORSKY

Patti Hawkins

Trinity | 2003

18 X 18 INCHES (45.7 X 45.7 CM)
Rattan, waxed linen, dye; hand dyed,
three-rod wale, broken twill, double
base, stake additions

PHOTO © BOYD-FITZGERALD, INC.

Rev. Wendy Ellsworth

Tanjung Danau | 2003

9½ X 6½ X 8 INCHES (24.1 X 16.5 X 20.3 CM)
Thread, glass seed beads, glass beads, wire; off-loom
bead weaving, herringbone stitch, gourd stitch

PHOTO © DAVID ELLSWORTH

Susan kavicky

Sitting II | 2005

18¼ X 18¼ X 7½ INCHES (46.4 X 46.4 X 19.1 CM)

Brown ash, foam-core form; plaited, twilled, double-walled construction

PHOTO © LARRY SANDERS

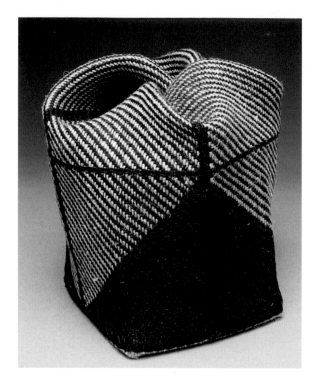

Kay Sekimachi

Untitled | 1997

6 X 5 INCHES DIAMETER (15.2 X 12.7 CM)

Hornet's nest paper

PHOTO © DAVID PETERS
COURTESY DEL MANO GALLERY

Dorothy McGuinness

Tuxedo | 2004

7 X 9 X 9 INCHES (17.8 X 22.9 X 22.9 CM)

Watercolor paper, acrylic paint, waxed linen, ribbon;
broken square twill start, diagonal-twill woven, sewn

PHOTO © KEN ROWE

Bird Ross

What 6,000 Looks Like | 2001

11 X 14 X 14 INCHES (27.9 X 35.6 X 35.6 CM)
Tape, lentils, split peas; constructed

PHOTOS © TOM MCINVAILLE

I WANTED *to know what 6,000 looked like. How can anyone possibly imagine what 6,000 of anything look like, let alone people. What would 6,000 names struck from the pages of a phone book look like? What would it look like in terms of their handprints, their footprints, in terms of the number of people that miss them? It's like nothing we can imagine. This was my attempt to imagine the loss of 9/11.*

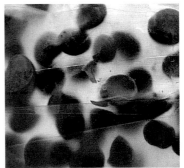

WITH THE *co-creation of my will and nature's, I honor the ultimate maker through the materials I collect in the forest.*

Jeanne Drevas

Vase Form II | 2002

13 X 10 INCHES (33 X 25.4 CM)
White-pine bark, long-leaf pine needles,
black-birch willow, waxed linen; sewn

PHOTO © ARTIST

Suzye Ogawa

Ikebana Vessel | 2004

2½ X 1⅛ X ¾ FEET
(76.2 X 34.3 X 22.9 CM)

Bronze, pink palm,
grapevine, silk; lost-wax
cast, twined, knotted

PHOTO © GEORGE POST

315

Phillip Sellers

Untitled | 2004

9½ X 8 INCHES (24.1 X 20.3 CM)
Stoneware, glaze, stain; woven,
sculpted, fired to cone 6
PHOTO © JERRY ANTHONY

CLAY IS *a medium that lends itself to many possibilities. Using it to weave clay baskets has been a challenge, but a rewarding one.*

Phillip Sellers

Untitled | 2005

15 X 8 INCHES (38.1 X 20.3 CM)
Stoneware, glaze, stain; woven, sculpted, fired to cone 6
PHOTO © PAUL LINHARES

Clay Burnette

Tribal | 2000

12 X 15 X 15 INCHES (30.5 X 38.1 X 38.1 CM)

Long-leaf pine needles, waxed-linen thread, beeswax; coiled construction

PHOTO © GEORGE FULTON

THESE TOOLS
with sheaths were
inspired by visits to
hardware stores,
antique shops, and
ethnological museums.

Danielle Bodine

Artifact Tools 7320 & 6664 | 2005

LARGEST: 20 X 4 X 2 INCHES (50.8 X 10.2 X 5.1 CM);
SMALLEST: 13 X 4 X 2 INCHES (33 X 10.2 X 5.1 CM)

Linen, mulberry paper, paper core, miner's pick,
metal pieces; coiled, covered with paper,
stamped, painted, burned

PHOTO © MICHAEL STADLER

Martha Monson Lowe

Chelan Sisters' Baskets | 2005

LARGEST: 18 X 11 X 6 INCHES (45.7 X 33 X 15.2 CM);
SMALLEST: 12 X 11 X 5 INCHES (30.5 X 33 X 12.7 CM)

Flat/oval rattan, seagrass, driftwood;
walnut dyed, plaited

PHOTO © LARRY SANDERS

Susan Goebel Dickman

Untitled | 1999

11½ X 7 X 6½ INCHES (29.2 X 17.8 X 16.5 CM)
Wild cherry bark and roots; plaited, twined
PHOTO © PETRONELLA YTSMA

Wendy Gadbois Jensen

Lidded Potbelly Urn | 2003

22 X 15 X 12 INCHES (55.9 X 38.1 X 30.5 CM)
Rattan; hand dyed, chase woven, braided
PHOTO © JEFF BAIRD

Jan Hopkins
Minerva | 2004

20 X 17 X 9 INCHES (50.8 X 43.2 X 22.9 CM)
Cherry bark, yellow-cedar bark, waxed linen; stitched and
woven bark, coiled with a looping technique

PHOTOS © WENDY MCEAHERN

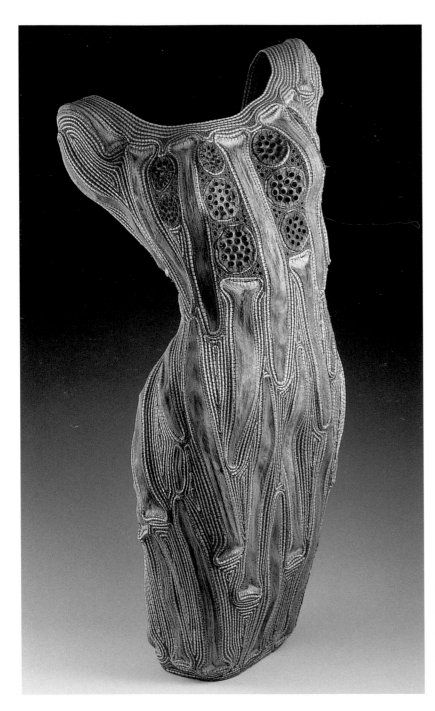

Jan Hopkins

Dance | 2004

35 X 16 X 12 INCHES (88.9 X 40.6 X 30.5 CM)

Agave leaves, lotus-pod tops, yellow-cedar bark, waxed linen; stitched, molded, coiled with a looping technique

PHOTO © JERRY MCCOLLUM

Cindy Wrobel

A Woman's Curves | 2004

7 X 5 X 4 INCHES (17.8 X 12.7 X 10.2 CM)

Beads, wire; strung, wrapped

PHOTO © JIM SOKOLIK

Suzy Wahl

Boxed In | 2000

3½ X 4 X 1 INCHES (8.9 X 10.2 X 2.5 CM)

Glass beads; netted beading

PHOTO © ARTIST

323

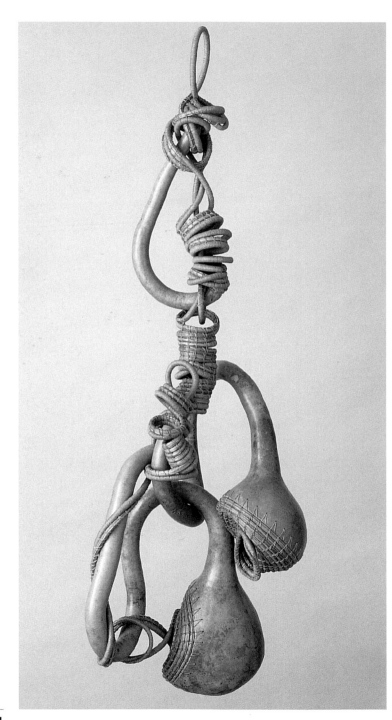

Peggy Wiedemann

Getting Started | 2004

31 X 9 X 12 INCHES (78.7 X 22.9 X 30.5 CM)
Gourds, pine needles, Irish waxed linen
PHOTO © BERNARD WOLF

IN GREEK *and Roman mythology, everyone entered the underworld after death by being placed on a boat to cross the River Styx. The rich had coins placed on their eyes, or in their hands, to pay the ferryman. The poor were forced to float in the current until they bumped into the other shore and found a resting place there.*

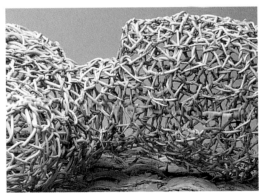

Carole Rouin

Crossing the River Styx | 2004

36 X 36 X 7 INCHES (91.4 X 91.4 X 17.8 CM)
Vine rattan, malacca bark, wire mesh, rebar;
random weave, over/under weave construction
PHOTO © BERNARD WOLF

Darryl Arawjo
Karen Arawjo
Lidded Light Vessel CLX | 2001

9 X 9 INCHES (22.9 X 22.9 CM)
White oak, hickory, monofilament, walnut, cherry;
hand split, carved, shaved, woven, lathe turned
PHOTO © DAVID W. COULTER

MY SCULPTURAL *work physically contains,
and visibly documents, obsessive and laborious
fiber-construction processes. I am increasingly
interested in exposing the insides/undersides that
are normally hidden from the viewer, as well as
continuing to formally explore the body, inside and
out, in more abstract terms.*

Daniel Evan Schwartz
Revisiting Analytic Tendencies | 2004

8 X 5 X 3 INCHES (20.3 X 12.7 X 7.6 CM)
Waxed-linen thread, fiber rush core; coiled
PHOTO © MICHAEL CAVANAGH

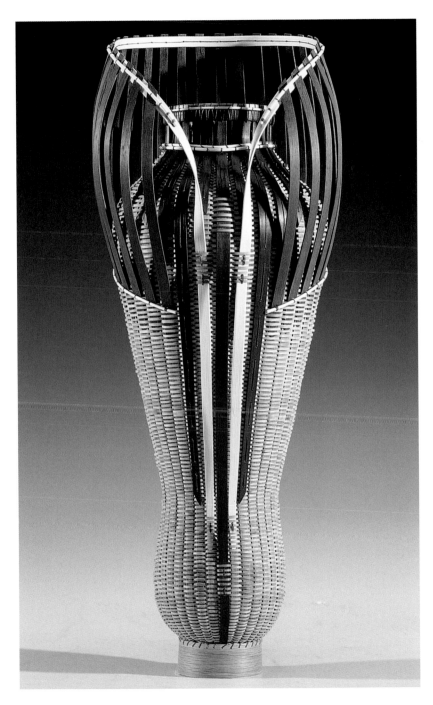

Leon Niehues

#44-04 | 2004

26 X 11 X 11 INCHES (66 X 27.9 X 27.9 CM)

Dyed and natural local white oak, coralberry runners, linen thread; split, woven free-form, drilled, stitched

PHOTO © SEAN MOORMAN

Kathy Doolittle

Shouldering the Journey | 2003

14 X 15 X 8 INCHES (35.6 X 38.1 X 20.3 CM)
Palm inflorescence, handmade paper,
gourd, waxed linen; coiled, woodburned
PHOTO © GEORGE POST

THIS PIECE *was created to depict the frustrations of my job. The evolving patterns and colors of the exterior are in direct contrast to the interior. The vivid yellow color is beginning to sneak out of the inner space since I have decided I can no longer be silent.*

Judy L. Kahle
I Will Not Be Silent | 2002

12 X 9 X 5 INCHES (30.5 X 22.9 X 12.7 CM)
Thread, hand-printed cotton, canvas;
machine stitched, collaged

PHOTOS © JERRY ANTHONY

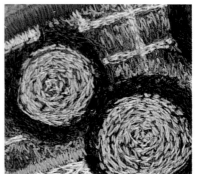

Ruth Greenberg
Untitled | 1995

4½ X 4½ X 3½ INCHES (11.4 X 11.4 X 8.9 CM)
Bindweed, driftwood
PHOTO © DAVID PETERS
COURTESY DEL MANO GALLERY

Rebecca McEntee
Pineapple | 2005

7¾ X 9 INCHES (19.7 X 22.9 CM)
Cotton, fiber-rush core; coiled
PHOTO © ARTIST

MY FORM *follows the waves of the driftwood and works downward to a grounded base.*

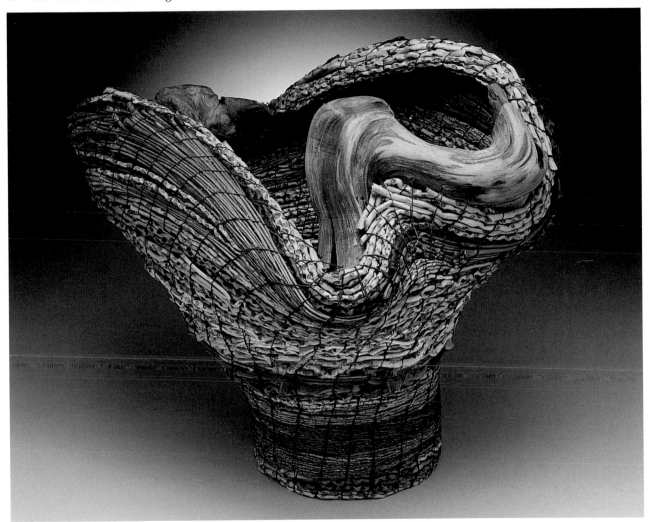

Gayna Uransky

Untitled | 2004

16 X 18 X 12 INCHES (40.6 X 45.7 X 30.5 CM)

Queen palm seed strands, jacaranda leaf stems, waxed
Irish linen thread, driftwood; hand dyed, coiled

PHOTO © GEORGE POST

THE CHALLENGE
of connecting a handle to this kind of piece is an engineering joy.

Stephen Kostyshyn
Handled Vessel | 2004

24 X 12 X 10 INCHES (61 X 30.5 X 25.4 CM)
Clay, smoked reed, willow, red osier, sumac; wheel thrown, altered, assembled, woven
PHOTO © ARTIST

Martha Monson Lowe

Herb's Chelan Wall Basket | 2003

47 X 24 X 8 INCHES (119.4 X 61 X 20.3 CM)

Rattan, seagrass, driftwood; walnut dyed, continuous weave

PHOTO © LARRY SANDERS

Cass Schorsch

Poncho for Sedona | 2005

11 X 6 X 3 INCHES (27.9 X 15.2 X 7.6 CM)
Birch bark, copper, cedar
PHOTO © TOM MCCOLLEY

Arlene K. McGonagle

Paradigm | 2004

8 X 9 X 9 INCHES (20.3 X 22.9 X 22.9 CM)
Paper, wire, waxed linen; plaited
PHOTO © JAMES BEARDS

THIS BASKET was inspired
by my feelings during my
teaching trip in the USA in the
fall of 2001. I would probably
not create something like this at
home in Russia. The fragment of
the basket is the bottom of it and
means: from top left, a rooster;
top right, sun, clouds, and water;
bottom left, ground and seeds,
and bottom right, moon.

Vladimir Yarish

The Basket for a Mouse, Three Birds, and a Man | 2001

17½ X 13½ INCHES (44.5 X 34.3 CM)

Birch bark, wood, fir-tree roots; double-woven construction

PHOTOS © ARTIST

STARRY, STARRY NIGHT
is one piece in a series
that explores the twill possibil-
ities in an eight-point pattern
that is based upon a quatrefoil
twill pattern found in antique
Shaker baskets.

JoAnn Kelly Catsos
Starry, Starry Night | 2004

3½ X 4¼ X 4¼ INCHES (8.9 X 10.8 X 10.8 CM)
Black-ash splint, maple, stain;
eight-point twill pattern, mold woven

PHOTOS © JEFF MAGIDSON

Joan Brink

Migration | 2003

13 X 10 INCHES (33 X 25.4 CM)

Reed, painted reed, bleached and dyed cane,
ebonized tropical walnut, Zuni blackbird in jet;
stake and strand construction, plain weave

PHOTOS © ERIC SWANSON

JoAnn Kelly Catsos

Rosebud | 2002

2 X 1⅞ X 1⅞ INCHES (5.1 X 4.7 X 4.7 CM)
Black-ash splint, dye; four- and
eight-point twill construction, mold woven

PHOTO © JEFF BAIRD

Wendy Gadbois Jensen

Twilled, Twined & Topped | 2005

14 X 11 X 8 INCHES (35.6 X 27.9 X 20.3 CM)
Rattan, black ash, round-reed; chase-woven
twill and twining rows, rolled border

PHOTO © JOHN POLAK

JoAnn Kelly Catsos

Cherry Jubilee | 2004

7 X 9 X 9 INCHES (17.8 X 24.1 X 24.1 CM)

Black-ash splint, maple, cherry stain; eight-point
twill construction, mold woven, hand shaped

PHOTOS © JEFF MAGIDSON

Joan Brink

Corn Circle | 2003

14 X 11 ¼ INCHES (35.6 X 28.6 CM)

Reed, natural and bleached cane, bloodwood; stake and strand construction, plain weave

PHOTO © ERIC SWANSON

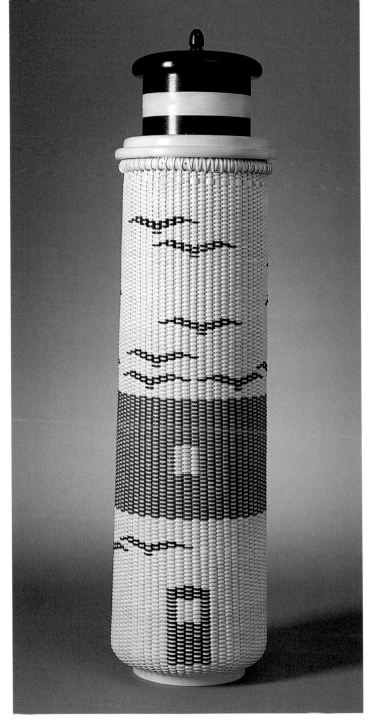

SANKATY LIGHT *is a representation of the lighthouse in the village of Siasconset, Massachusetts, where I spent summers as I was growing up. I used the Nantucket lightship basket technique to weave one of the icons of that island.*

Joan Brink

Sankaty Light | 2002

24 X 5¾ INCHES (61 X 14.6 CM)

Reed, dyed and bleached cane, ebony and holly lantern and base; stake and strand construction, plain weave

PHOTO © ERIC SWANSON

THIS BASKET *was made to show a new technique that I call "surfacing." The black pine needles are on the front only. The back of the basket is all sweetgrass and is as perfect as the front.*

Martha Van Meter

Masters Basket | 2003

11 X 12 X 1¼ INCHES (27.9 X 30.5 X 3.2 CM)
South Carolina sweetgrass, pine needles,
agate set in resin, faux sinew; dyed, sewn
PHOTO © ARTIST

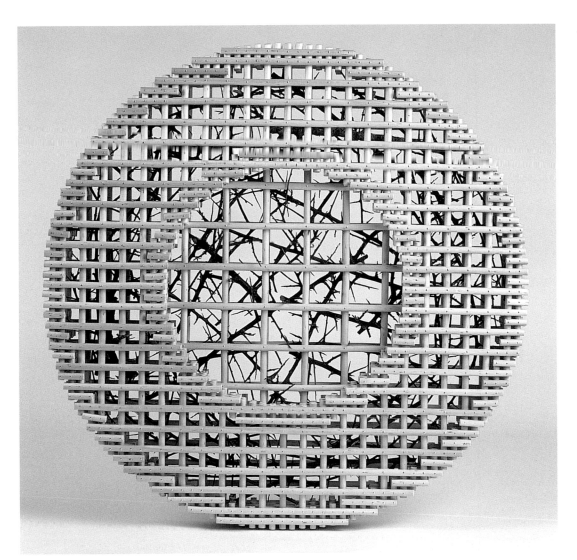

Dail Behennah

Dish with Blackthorn | 2004

3⅛ X 24 X 24 INCHES (8 X 61 X 61 CM)

Willow, silver-plated pins, blackthorn;
drilled, constructed

PHOTOS © JASON INGRAM

Judy A. Zugish

Emergence: Many Moods, Many Moons | 2004

11 X 3 X 4 INCHES (27.9 X 7.6 X 10.2 CM)

Peeled willow skins, hand-skinned willow rods; plaited, molded, stitched, constructed with one continuous piece of willow bark

PHOTO © JERRY MCCOLLUM

Dorothy Gill Barnes

Ginkgo | 1991

15 X 11 X 13 INCHES (38.1 X 27.9 X 33 CM)

Ginkgo bark

PHOTO © DOUG MARTIN
COURTESY DEL MANO GALLERY

Martha Monson Lowe

Tall Chelan Basket | 2003

35 X 16 X 12 INCHES (88.9 X 40.6 X 30.5 CM)

Rattan, seagrass, cane, vine rattan,
driftwood; walnut dyed, plaited, twined,
3-rod wale

PHOTO © LARRY SANDERS

Lanny Bergner

Airium | 2004

38 X 16 X 16 INCHES (96.5 X 40.6 X 40.6 CM)
Gourd, bronze screen, bb shot, wire;
burned, hand connected, glued, wrapped

PHOTO © WILLIAM WICKETT

Leon Niehues

#77-02 | 2002

27 X 14 X 14 INCHES (68.6 X 35.6 X 35.6 CM)

Dyed and natural local white oak, coralberry runners, waxed-linen thread; woven free form, split, drilled, stitched

PHOTOS © MICHAEL CROW

Jan W. Henry

Quilter's Sewing Basket | 2003

10¼ X 12¼ X 10¼ INCHES (26 X 31.1 X 26 CM)

White oak, black walnut, maple, cherry, embroidery floss, muslin; fabricated, wood burning, twill weaving, woodworking, parquetry, woven, laminated, fabric dyed, hand sewn

PHOTOS © ARTIST

Jan W. Henry
World Peace | 2002

8½ X 8½ X 8½ INCHES (21.6 X 21.6 X 21.6 CM)

Black walnut, cherry, maple, holly, white oak, leather; oak rod and splint making, twill weaving, woodworking, carved

PHOTO © ARTIST

THE BASES *are cherry burl. Although a more brittle wood, cherry was steam bent for the handles so that they complemented the burl bases.*

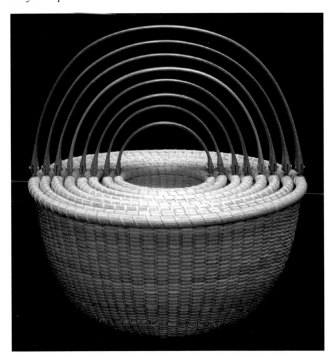

Claudia Leo
Nest of Eight Nantuckets | 1999

4 TO 12 INCHES DIAMETER (10.2 TO 30.5 CM)

Cherry, cherry burl, ash staves, cane; mold woven

PHOTO © ARTIST

Fran Reed

Body Politic | 2004

25 X 17 X 12 INCHES (63.5 X 43.2 X 30.5 CM)

Salmon skin, gut, bamboo; stitched

PHOTO © CHRIS AREND

THE USE *of ordinary household items and the unfinished form of the work references the Japanese aesthetic of wabi sabi— imperfection, incompleteness, humble and unconventional materials.*

Jacy Diggins

Wood Sprite's Vase | 2003

17 X 7 X 14 INCHES (43.2 X 17.8 X 35.6 CM)

Natural waxed paper, tea bags, indigo, rust, thread, wire base; pleated, dyed, rusted, tied

PHOTOS © LAUREL HUNGERFORD

Shirl Parmentier

Jim Parmentier

Fruit Basket | 2004

12 X 21 X 8 INCHES (30.5 X 53.3 X 20.3 CM)

Stoneware, ash glaze; slab built, extruded, coiled; reduction fired to cone 10

PHOTO © RALPH GABRINER

Catherine L. Siterlet

Stability | 2001

11 X 9 X 7 INCHES (27.9 X 22.9 X 17.8 CM)
Cedar bark, rattan, leather; plain weave, twined
PHOTO © ARTIST

Shirl Parmentier
Jim Parmentier

Flower Basket | 2004

16 X 12 INCHES (40.6 X 30.5 CM)
Stoneware, ash glaze; slab built, extruded,
coiled, reduction fired to cone 10
PHOTO © RALPH GABRINER

MY VESSELS *are a continuing exploration to meld hard and soft materials.*

Suzye Ogawa

Well | 2003

1½ X 1¾ X 1 FEET (45.7 X 53.3 X 30.5 CM)

Bronze, palm inflorescence, silk;
lost-wax cast, coiled

PHOTO © GEORGE POST

Mary Hettmansperger

Directions | 2004

12 X 6 X 6 INCHES (30.5 X 15.2 X 15.2 CM)
Black ash, honeysuckle; twill woven
PHOTO © JEFF BAIRD

Christine Love Adcock

Hiccup Basket | 2005

14 X 12½ INCHES (35.6 X 31.8 CM)
Dyed palm fiber; coiled
PHOTO © MEHOSH DZIADZIO

Christine Love Adcock

Jacaranda Basket | 2004

10 X 14 INCHES (25.4 X 35.6 CM)
Dyed date-palm inflorescence,
jacaranda seed pods; coiled, woven
PHOTO © MEHOSH DZIADZIO

Cass Schorsch

Stray Cat | 2004

11 X 9 INCHES (27.9 X 22.9 CM)

Birch bark, rattan, cedar

PHOTOS © LARRY SANDERS

June Jasen

Floating Fish in the Palm Vessel Basket | 2005

3⅝ X 4¾ X 4½ INCHES (9.2 X 12.1 X 11.4 CM)

Copper-wire cloth, vitreous enamel, ceramic decals, luster glaze; fused

PHOTO © ARTIST

June Jasen

Baby M Floating By in a Basket | 2005

4 X 4 INCHES (10.2 X 10.2 CM)

Copper cloth, enamel, transfer stencil, 24-karat gold leaf; fused

PHOTO © ARTIST

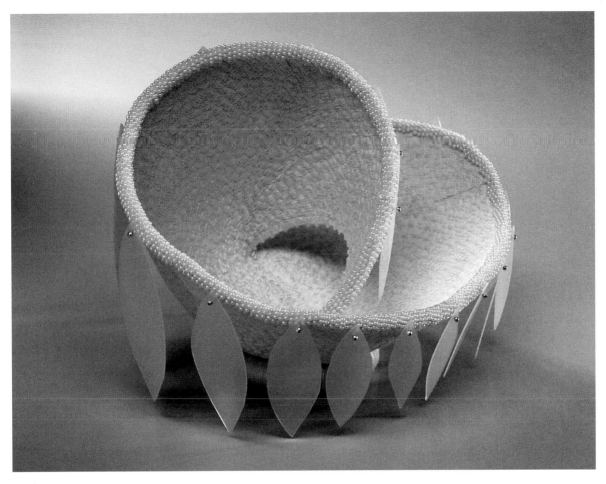

Robinsunne

Uncurling from the Ache; Surrounded by Beauty | 2004

6 X 8 X 6 INCHES (15.2 X 20.3 X 15.2 CM)

Fabric, thread, glass beads, 14-karat gold-filled beads, plastic trash;
machine quilted, hand sewn

PHOTO © WILLIAM THUSS

THE COLOR *and form of this basket are inspired by the striations of the jasper beads that are woven into it. The versatility of copper wire allows me to explore shapes that depart from traditional basketry, and to impart a sculptural quality to my work.*

K. Chrysalis

Jasper | 2005

3½ X 15¾ X 21⅝ INCHES (9 X 40 X 55 CM)

Electrical and telephone wire, leopard jasper, copper, seed beads; coiled, combined stitches with lashing, bound rim

PHOTO © BOB KITT

Scott Schuldt

Prairie Basket | 2004

20 X 5 INCHES (50.8 X 12.7 CM)

Barbed wire, deerskin, glass beads; plaited, sewn

PHOTO © ARTIST

Rosalie Friis-Ross

Summer | 2001

3 X 7 X 7 INCHES (7.6 X 17.8 X 17.8 CM)
Bias-plaited Japanese papers, katazome
(old kimono patterns), kozo

PHOTO © DAVID PETERS
COURTESY DEL MANO GALLERY

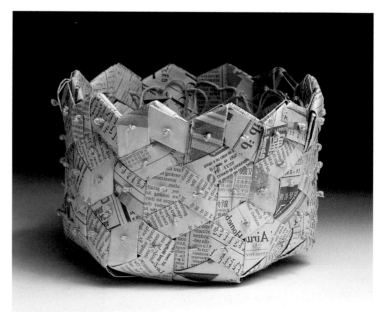

Carol D. Westfall

Pink Globally III | 2005

4½ X 7 INCHES (11.4 X 17.8 CM)
International newspapers,
cotton floss; hexagonally plaited

PHOTO © D. JAMES DEE

Leandra Spangler

And Then...Dawn | 2004

19 X 9 X 9 INCHES (48.3 X 22.9 X 22.9 CM)

Reed, handmade paper, glass
and metal beads, paint

PHOTO © HELIOS STUDIO

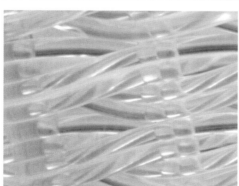

Martha H. Keller

Meditation | 1993

7½ X 13½ INCHES (19.1 X 34.3 CM)
Round reed, natural and clear monofiliment;
twined, three-rod wale technique

PHOTOS © JAY BEEBE

Ema Tanigaki

Summer Squash Basket with Standing Base | 2005

16 X 9 X 6 INCHES (40.6 X 22.9 X 15.2 CM)

Silicon bronze, bronze wire; hand wrought, welded, drilled, attached,
hand-formed, tendril weave technique, patinated, lacquered, waxed

PHOTO © JOHN L. HEALEY

I USE *earthy imagery— vegetative growth, tendril, flower, fruit, and seed—to connect my work with the traditional uses for baskets, as has been seen daily in agriculture and domestic life for many millennia. Traditional bronze baskets are a very ancient* mingei *form (folk art, or literal translation: people's art, in Japanese) and, to me, have always simultaneously evoked the primitive Bronze Age and the refinement of apprentice-based craftsmanship found in the Far East.*

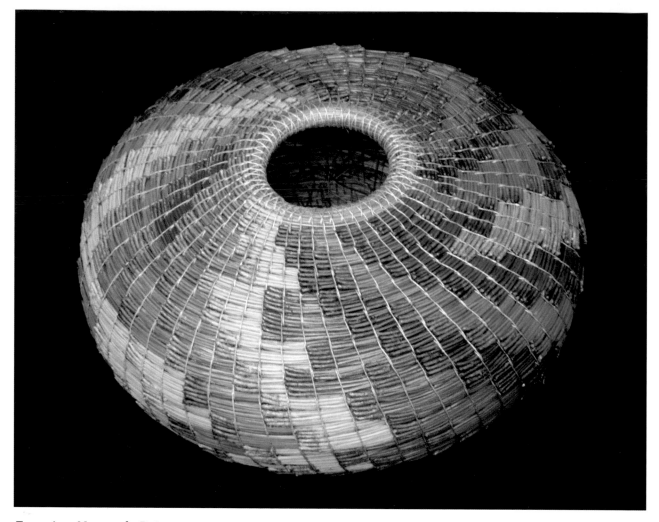

Francina Krayneh-Prince
Neil Prince

Diurnal Rise | 2004

12 X 18 X 18 INCHES (30.5 X 45.7 X 45.7 CM)
Torrey pine needles, waxed-linen cord, raffia;
dyed, coiled construction

PHOTO © ARTIST

Patti Lechman

Nikko | 2003

6 X 4 X 22 INCHES (15.2 X 10.2 X 5.1 CM)

Nylon, glass beads; knotted

PHOTO © DAVID PETERS
COURTESY DEL MANO GALLERY

Patti Lechman

Bamboo and Enso | 2003

6 X 4 X 2 INCHES (15.2 X 10.2 X 5.1 CM)

Nylon and glass beads; knotted

PHOTO © ARTIST

THIS WORK *was commissioned by a teapot collector. I loved the challenge of making a teapot, while keeping the organic feel of my baskets.*

Angie Harbin

Garden Teapot | 2003

13 X 8 X 6 INCHES
(33 X 20.3 X 15.2 CM)

Nylon, epoxy resin, paint, wax

PHOTO © MARGO GEIST

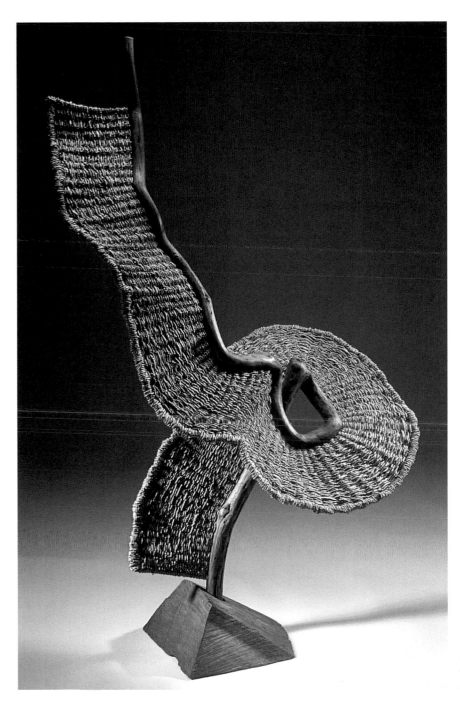

Don Weeke

Twist of Fate | 2005

52 X 31 X 18 INCHES
(132.1 X 78.7 X 45.7 CM)

Oak branch, rattan, palm
frond, eucalyptus; woven

PHOTO © RODNEY NAKAMOTO

Linda Fifield

Heaven & Earth | 2003

9½ X 5 X 5 INCHES (24.1 X 12.7 X 12.7 CM)
Czech glass beads, nylon thread,
wood form, netting; stitched

PHOTO © JACK FIFIELD

THE PROCESS *of manipulating colored threads to cover a three-dimensional form not only satisfies my creative spirit but allows me to express my love of fibers in a sculptural way.*

Jóh Ricci

Seafoam | 2004

2⅛ X 3½ INCHES (5.4 X 8.9 CM)
Nylon; hand dyed, knotted

PHOTO © T. R. WAILLES

Joyce Shannon

BK #356: Fly Fishing | 2003

21 X 18 X 18 INCHES (53.3 X 45.7 X 45.7 CM)
Raffia, round reed, beads, buttons; coiled

PHOTO © ARTIST

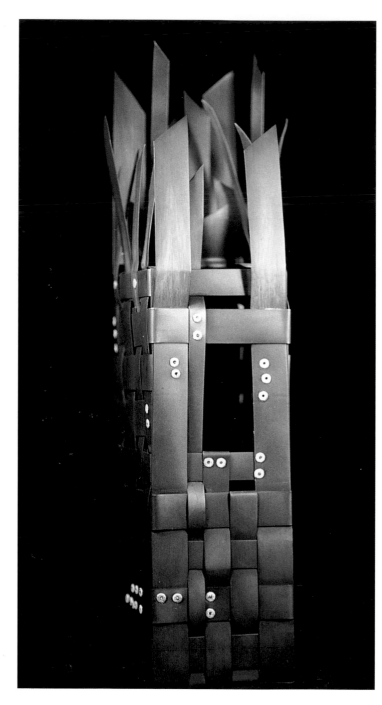

Anika Smulovitz

Burning House | 1998

18¼ X 4 X 5 INCHES (47.6 X 10.2 X 12.7 CM)
Copper, patina, colored pencils
PHOTO © ARTIST

THE INTERTWINING
and lyricism of clay
and fiber give this piece
its ethereal form.

Susan Fox Hirschmann

Ode to the Orioles Basket | 2004

42 X 12 X 8 INCHES (106.7 X 30.5 X 20.3 CM)

Porcelain, hand-dyed natural reeds, bamboo, hand-pounded black ash; carved, thrown, airbrushed, woven, continuous construction

PHOTO © JERRY ANTHONY

Barbara Walker

Les Pétales | 2002

2¾ X 12 X 5½ INCHES (7 X 30.5 X 14 CM)

Four-ply bleached and unbleached linen
cords made by artist; ply-split, wrapped

PHOTO © BRIAN MCLERNON

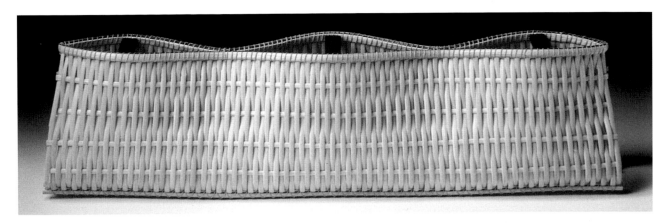

Tressa Sularz

Trois Rivieres | 2004

5¼ X 6 X 19½ INCHES (13.3 X 15.2 X 49.5 CM)
Natural reed, waxed linen, recycled mahogany
wood spacers; woven, wrapped
PHOTO © PETER LEE

Tressa Sularz

Apt | 2004

4½ X 7 X 17 INCHES (11.4 X 17.8 X 43.2 CM)
Natural reed, waxed linen; wrapped rim
and base supports
PHOTO © PETER LEE

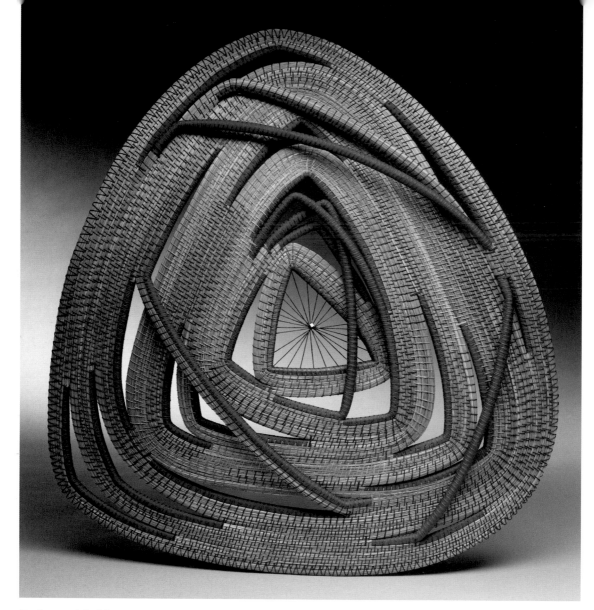

Debora Muhl

Sunset # 1227 | 2005

21½ X 20 X 3 INCHES (54.6 X 50.8 X 7.6 CM)

Maine sweetgrass, rayon ribbon,
waxed Irish linen; coiled

PHOTO © JOHN STERLING RUTH

Debora Muhl

Autumn Spirals # 1228 | 2005

11 X 12 X 9½ INCHES (27.9 X 30.5 X 24.1 CM)

Maine sweetgrass, nylon ribbon, waxed Irish linen; coiled

PHOTO © JOHN STERLING RUTH

Debora Muhl

Blue Aussie # 1229 | 2005

15¾ X 16 X 14 INCHES (40 X 40.6 X 35.6 CM)

Maine sweetgrass, rayon ribbon, waxed Irish linen; coiled

PHOTO © JOHN STERLING RUTH

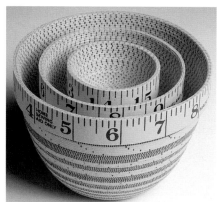

Karyl Sisson

Mixing Bowls | 2003

SMALLEST: 1¼ X 2 INCHES DIAMETER (4.4 X 5 CM);
LARGEST: 3⅛ X 4⅜ INCHES DIAMETER (7.9 X 11.1 CM)

Old cloth tape measures, polymer; coiled

PHOTOS © SUSAN EINSTEIN

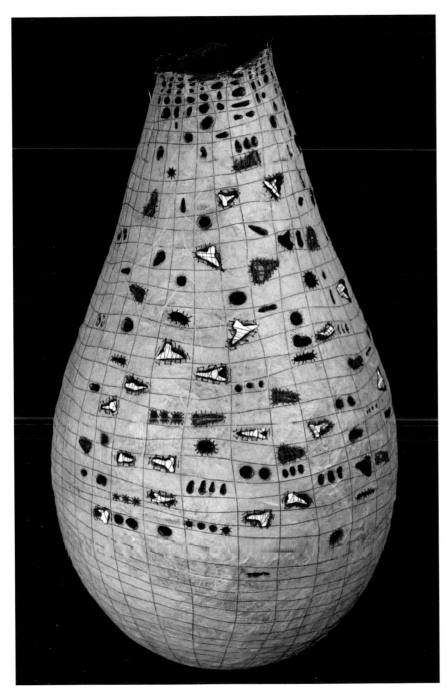

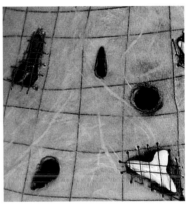

Diane Banks

Tribute to a Shark | 2002

12 X 20 INCHES (30.5 X 50.8 CM)
Rice paper, thread, dye, shark teeth
PHOTOS © ARTIST

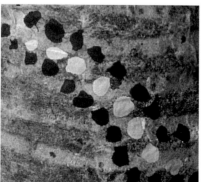

Helen Frost Way

Story Basket I | 2004

10 X 6 INCHES (25.4 X 15.2 CM)

Cotton fiber; coiled, collaged, painted

PHOTOS © RON MCCOY

Jo Stealey

Ancestral Relic | 2003

13 X 7 X 2 INCHES (33 X 17.8 X 5.1 CM)
Waxed linen, porcupine quills, sticks,
handmade paper; coiled

PHOTOS © PETER ANGER

THIS WAS *a short series designed with one gallery in mind. I wanted something shaped like my Japanese jars, but in vivid color.*

Nancy Moore Bess

Color, COLOR, Color | 2004

4 1/2 X 4 X 4 INCHES (11.4 X 10.2 X 10.2 CM)
Waxed linen and cotton,
Chinese incense-box lid; twined
PHOTO © D. JAMES DEE

Elaine Small

Autumn Interlude | 1999

6 1/2 X 5 1/4 X 4 3/8 INCHES (16.5 X 13.3 X 11.1 CM)
Waxed linen, beads; knotted
PHOTO © RED ELF

Arlene K. McGonagle
One Night | 2004

11 X 9½ X 6 INCHES (27.9 X 24.1 X 15.2 CM)
Paper, silk, wire, waxed linen, tapestry; plaited
PHOTOS © JAMES BEARDS

Kay Kahn

The Hitch | 2005

16¼ X 26 X 21 INCHES (41.3 X 66 X 53.3 CM)

Silk, cotton; quilted, pieced, appliquéd,
hand and machine stitched, constructed

PHOTO © WENDY MCEAHERN

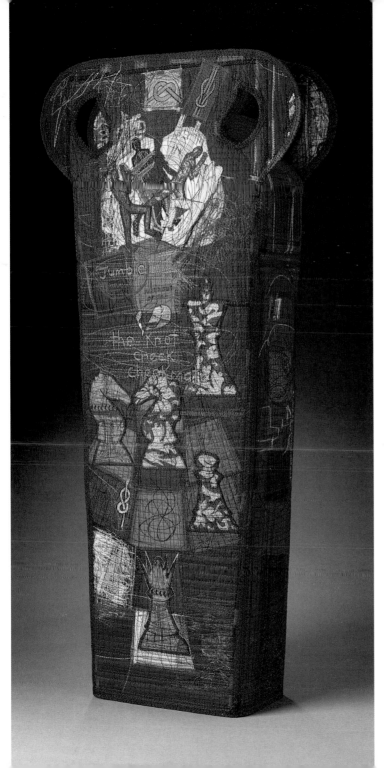

Kay Kahn

The Knot | 2005

35 X 16¼ X 6 INCHES (88.9 X 41.3 X 15.2 CM)

Silk, cotton; quilted, pieced, appliquéd,
hand and machine stitched, constructed

PHOTO © WENDY MCEAHERN

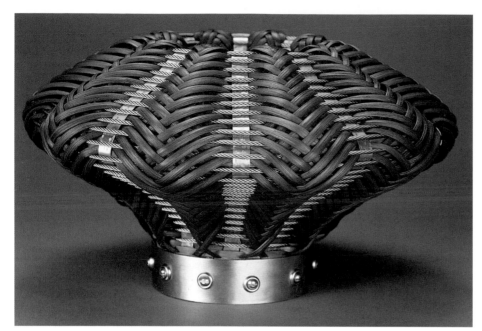

Carole Hetzel

Brendan #176 | 2004

10 X 18 X 18 INCHES (25.4 X 45.7 X 45.7 CM)
Hand-dyed rust reed, brass strips,
stainless-steel cable, brass base;
soldered, bolted, double-woven
continuous construction

PHOTO © ALLAN CARLISLE

Ruth Boland

Curves and Stripes | 2001
12 X 8 X 8 INCHES (30.5 X 20.3 X 20.3 CM)
Reed; hand dyed, start-stop construction

PHOTO © ARTIST

Carole Hetzel

Brendan #178 | 2004

20 X 18 X 18 INCHES (50.8 X 45.7 X 45.7 CM)

Hand-dyed reed, copper strips, copper
coupling, stainless-steel cable; double-woven
continuous construction

PHOTO © ALLAN CARLISLE

MY INSPIRATION *for* Ancient Myths *came from ancient Egyptian vessels. This piece looks like old tarnished metal and needs to be touched to believe that it is not. It looks as though it came from an ancient tomb.*

Patti Quinn Hill
Ancient Myths | 2004

17 X 13 INCHES (43.2 X 33 CM)
Cotton archival paper, acrylic paint, maple base, metallic thread; hand painted, continuous construction, curl embellishments

Shuji Ikeda

Tsuchi-Kago | 2004

12 X 12 X 12 INCHES (30.5 X 30.5 X 30.5 CM)

Slab and hand-built clay; braided

PHOTO © RICHARD SARGENT

John McQueen

Big Fly Basket | 2003

19 X 14 X 14 INCHES (48.3 X 35.6 X 35.6 CM)

Bark, sticks, string

PHOTO © ARTIST
COURTESY OF DEL MANO GALLERY

Mark Caluneo

Basket No. 7 | 2002

12 X 15 INCHES (30.5 X 38.1 CM)

Brass and copper sheet, copper wire, steel, patina, pigment; hammer textured, coiled, twist-tied construction technique, woven

PHOTOS © PETER SAN CHIRICO

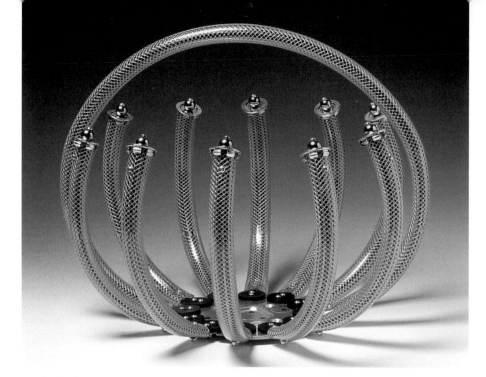

Rob Dobson

Basket #143 | 2004

13 X 16 X 15 INCHES (33 X 40.6 X 38.1 CM)

Garden hose, steel electrical plate, aluminum parts, knockout covers, chrome-plated plastic beads; constructed

PHOTO © JEFF BAIRD

Darryl Arawjo
Karen Arawjo

Verde Nuevo | 2004

11 X 7½ INCHES (27.9 X 19 CM)

Hickory, monofilament, ash, crystal flash; hand split, carved, shaved, woven

PHOTO © DAVID W. COULTER

Mary Merkel-Hess

Windblown | 2004

25 X 17 X 8 INCHES (63.5 X 43.2 X 20.3 CM)
Reed, paper, acrylic paint, papier-mâché
PHOTO © ARTIST

VESSEL MAKING *is as old as the need to gather and carry. Executed in fiber, stone, clay, metal, or glass, vessels are more than form or function. Each carries a visual history of influences and the whispered intention of its creator. Grand or intimate, mundane or precious, vessels are both object and metaphor.*

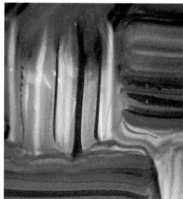

Richard Moiel
Katherine Poeppel
Untitled | 2002

13½ X 5½ X 5½ INCHES (34.3 X 14 X 14 CM)
Blown glass; murrine/incalmo
technique, acid etched
PHOTOS © ARTIST

Richard Moiel
Katherine Poeppel
Untitled | 2003

10 X 6 X 6 INCHES (25.4 X 15.2 X 15.2 CM)
Blown glass; murrine/incalmo
technique, acid etched

PHOTOS © ARTIST

Jill Powers

A Change in Direction | 2005

15 X 20 X 12 INCHES (38.1 X 50.8 X 30.5 CM)
Bark fiber, waxed linen; cooked, manipulated,
cast, dyed, stitched

PHOTO © DON MURRAY

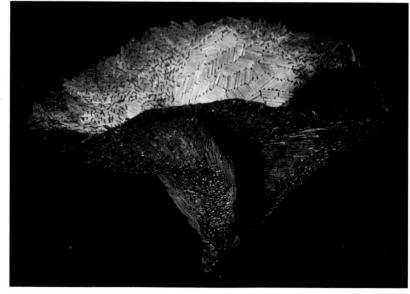

Diane Banks

Century | 1998

10¼ X 8¼ INCHES (26 X 21 CM)
Wood, wire, paper, dye

PHOTO © ARTIST

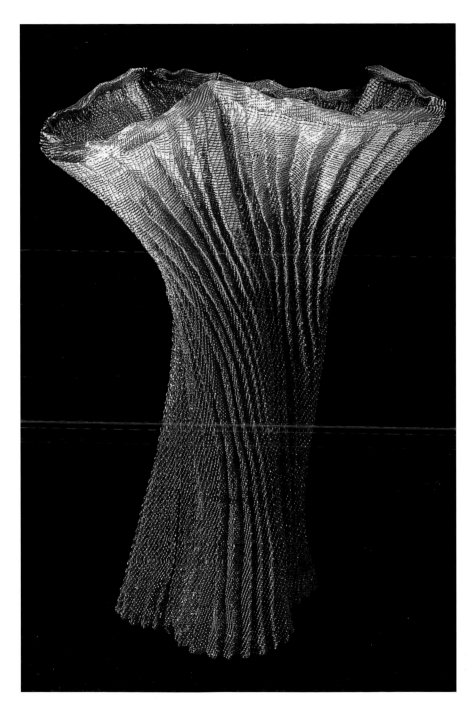

Donna Kaplan

Heat Wave | 2003

17 X 11 X 8 INCHES
(43.2 X 27.9 X 20.3 CM)

Wire, rayon thread;
loom woven, sewn, sculpted

PHOTOS © JERRY MCCOLLUM

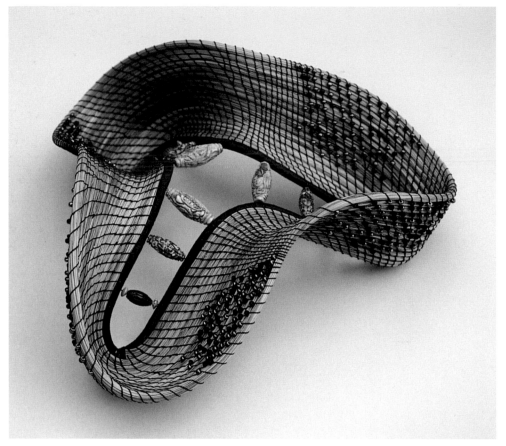

OVER THE *years, my work has evolved from traditional-shaped vessels to a more sculptural style that reflects my creative and spiritual journey. Coiling baskets is a process that offers so many gifts—it calms, nurtures, and satisfies. My current work embraces motion and frequently has windows for the viewer to see inside, where sometimes there is a stone waiting to be seen.*

Nadine Spier

Connections | 2005

5 X 13 X 12 INCHES (12.7 X 33 X 30.5 CM)
Pine needles, picture jasper,
leopard jasper, beads,
waxed-linen thread; coiled

K. Chrysalis

Electra | 2003

4⅓ X 15¾ X 16½ INCHES (11 X 40 X 42 CM)

Electrical and telephone wire, silver and glass
beads; coiled base with twined sides, frayed
beaded ends, assembled

PHOTOS © BOB KITT

MY BASKETS *are lined with beads on their interior, as a metaphor for the beauty that is within us, and within all creatures.*

Krista Spieler

Red | 2003

3 X 4½ INCHES (7.6 X 11.4 CM)
Waxed linen, hemp-twine core, seed beads;
coiled basketry construction, stitched
PHOTO © PETER LEE

Rev. Wendy Ellsworth

Teluk Semangka | 2002

5¼ X 6¼ X 4½ INCHES (12.7 X 15.9 X 11.4 CM)
Thread, glass seed beads, coral,
clay modeling compound; off-loom weaving,
herringbone stitch, gourd stitch
PHOTO © DAVID ELLSWORTH

Sharon Meyer Postance

Moon Series | 2002

14 X 21 X 8 INCHES (35.6 X 53.3 X 20.3 CM)

Paper, sisal, brass wire; papier-mâché

PHOTO © ARTIST

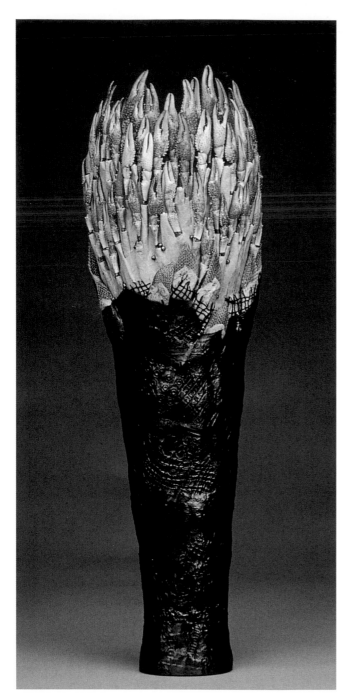

Leandra Spangler

One Hundred Hands Clapping | 2004

23 X 6½ X 6½ INCHES (58.4 X 16.5 X 16.5 CM)

Reed, handmade paper, crawfish claws, copper foil, wire, copper and nematite beads, copper brads, copper wire mesh, ping-pong netting, joss paper, graphite emulsion

PHOTOS © HELIOS STUDIO

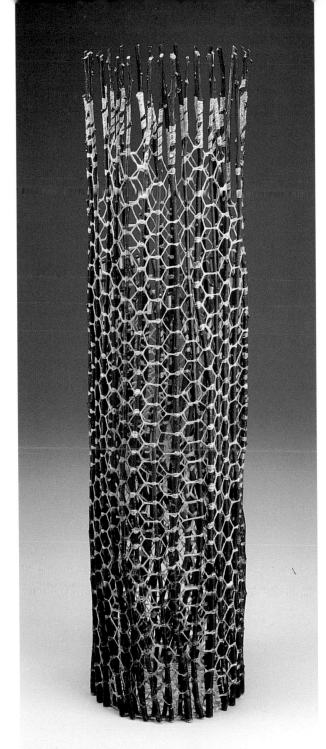

NIGHT AFTER *night on the evening news, the TV networks showed footage of devastating, uncontrolled California forest fires. Red flames silhouetted against a black sky.*

Jill Nordfors Clark

Fire in the Night Sky | 2003

27½ X 6½ INCHES (69.9 X 16.5 CM)

Hog gut, plum twigs, parachute cord; double layered, dyed, stitched

PHOTOS © TOM HOLT

Andrea Tucker-Holly
Untitled | 2003

9 X 3¼ X 2½ INCHES (22.9 X 8.3 X 6.4 CM)
Flax, hand-dyed camel and kozo hair,
brass base; drape molded
PHOTO © ARTIST

Kay Sekimachi
Untitled | 2000

9 X 7 X 7 INCHES (22.9 X 17.8 X 177.8 CM)
Linen; double-weave twill tabby
PHOTO © DAVID PETERS
COURTESY DEL MANO GALLERY

Luce Robineau

Confluence | 2003

12 X 6 INCHES (30.5 X 15.2 CM)

Paper from hornet's nest, acrylic paint, feathers, willow

PHOTO © PAUL SIMON

Vicki Vigée

Untitled | 2005

8 X 9 X 9 INCHES (20.3 X 22.9 X 22.9 CM)
Silk, printed paper, poplar; hand woven
PHOTO © STEVE MANN

Erna van Overbeek-Sanders

Spiderweb Basket | 2005

6⁵⁄₁₆ X 7⁷⁄₈ X 4¾ INCHES (16 X 20 X 12 CM)
Copper wire; woven, electroformed, enameled
PHOTO © GREGORY R. STALEY

John McGuire

Gridwork | 2001

11 X 12 X 14 INCHES (27.9 X 30.5 X 35.6 CM)

Black ash, golden rod stems, waxed-linen cord

PHOTO © DAVID PETERS
COURTESY DEL MANO GALLERY

Tom Muir

Please Do Not Touch the Artwork | 2004

18 X 34 X 18 INCHES (45.7 X 86.4 X 45.7 CM)

Honey locust, sycamore, copper,
insect egg cases; woven, stapled, riveted

PHOTO © TIM THAYER

Mick Luehrman

Somebody Lives Here | 2000

15 X 14 X 12 INCHES (38.1 X 35.6 X 30.5 CM)
Honey locust, barbed wire, wire,
etched copper; coiled, random weave

PHOTOS © PETE ANGER

AS AN *elementary-school art teacher, I was saddened to realize that some of my students had to grow up in "thorny nests." This thorn basket serves as a metaphor for these not-so-cozy homes that some children have to endure.*

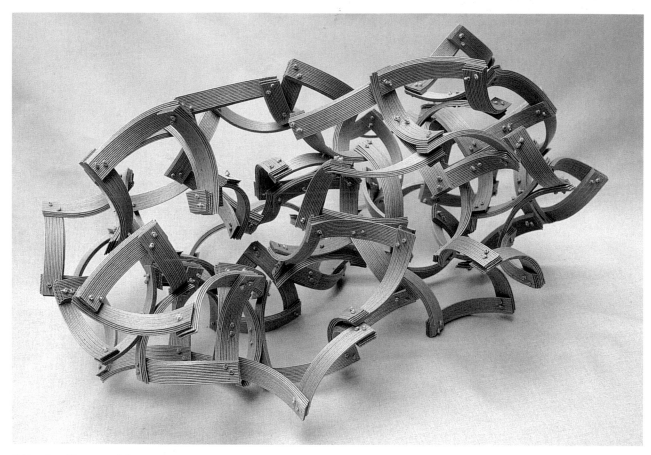

Ritsuko Jinnouchi

Heptagon Structure Basket #3 | 2004

10⅝ X 19¹¹⁄₁₆ X 11¹³⁄₁₆ INCHES (27 X 50 X 30 CM)

Paper band, paper string; connected

Gyöngy Laky

Standing Vessel | 2001

16 X 16 X 16 INCHES (40.6 X 40.6 X 40.6 CM)
Plum prunings, drywall bullets; screwed
PHOTO © M. LEE FATHERREE

Polly Jacobs Giacchina

Finding The Way | 2005

15 X 19 X 21 INCHES (38.1 X 48.3 X 53.3 CM)
Bamboo wangi (root), washi paper;
heat-bent assemblage, collaged
PHOTO © RODNEY NAKAMOTO

About the Juror

Jan Peters is co-owner of del Mano Gallery in West Los Angeles, California. Since 1973, she and partner Ray Leier have been exhibiting and promoting fine contemporary craft art. The gallery annually hosts five major group exhibitions and several one-person shows in the major craft fields, with a focus on fiber objects, mixed media, and turned and sculptured wood.

Jan and her partner, along with well-known writer and curator Kevin Wallace, have collaborated on a series of gallery-style books on craft art. Thus far, the series includes *Contemporary Turned Wood: New Perspectives in a Rich Tradition; Contemporary Glass: Color, Light & Form;* and *Baskets: Tradition and Beyond.*

She has been a juror many times for national craft shows, including the American Craft Council Show, the Philadelphia Museum of Art Craft Show, and the Smithsonian Craft Show, as well as a lecturer at basket and wood symposiums.

Jan currently serves on the boards of the National Basketry Organization, the Glass Alliance of Los Angeles, and the Collectors of Wood Art. In 2004 she, Ray, and Kevin juried *500 Wood Bowls.*

Acknowledgments

Thank you to the many talented artists who sent us images of their outstanding basket creations. This book would not have been possible without your collective talent and desire to share your work.

A big thank you to Jan Peters, who honored us by taking time from her busy schedule to jury the submissions for this collection. Her diligent attention to details is all the more admirable considering she handled the entire jurying process herself, and did it long distance from California. Much of the credit for this book goes to you, Jan.

Jan told us she relied on the assistance of her staff, especially Christina Carroll for keeping everything organized for her, and Kirsten Muenster for her keen eye. She credits several people for giving her great advice, perspective, and support—her husband David Peters, her partner Ray Leier, Michael Davis, Judy Mulford, Rosalie Friis Ross, Lloyd Cotsen, and Kevin Wallace. Jan and I would both like to thank Anne Gochenour, Curator of Contemporary Craft, Arkansas Arts Center, for supplying images of work from the museum's collection for the introduction.

Thanks also to Louise Hamby who, through her commitment to the basketmaking communities of Arnhem Land, Australia, submitted several images of Gapuwiyak traditional fiber baskets by. Louise heard about 500 Baskets through Object Gallery in Sydney, and we are delighted that some pieces were juried into this collection.

And, to my highly talented co-workers here at Lark Books, my sincere gratitude for all your support and help in preparing this book for publication.

Susan Kieffer

Contributing Artists